Sylvia Boorstein's *It's Easier Than You Think*

"Endearingly personal grandmotherly mindfulness wisdom in doses that slide right into the heart, dissolving our most debilitating fears and illusions with kindness, clarity, and gentle humor. If you want to expand your understanding of mindfulness and deepen (and maybe even loosen up) your meditation practice, then read this wonderful book!"   –Jon Kabat-Zinn, author of *Wherever You Go, There You Are*

"Sylvia Boorstein builds a magical bridge from everyday life to the ancient wisdom of the Buddha. The simplicity and directness of her writing does not disguise its deep design–out of kindness to all, she has mastered the art of the teaching story, making old truths shine new."   –Rodger Kamenetz, author of *The Jew in the Lotus*

"Sylvia's simple clear seeing clears simple seeing for us all. Hers is Grandma Dharma–a soft, persevering of the heart toward the place we each took birth to discover. Read it to your grandmother, practice it with your grandchildren, be it."
     –Stephen Levine, co-author of *Embracing the Beloved*

"A unique and charming book! Sylvia Boorstein's Buddhism is as real as it is spiritual."   –Marion Woodman, author of *The Ravaged Bridegroom*

"In the Theravadin Buddhist tradition the word for teacher is 'Kalyana Mitta,' or spiritual friend. A spiritual friend is recognized by their wisdom, lightness of heart, grace in adversity, and notable compassion. . . . Sylvia Boorstein is a true 'Kalyana Mitta,' who has served many through her teaching and now through this book. Her voice is the voice of a remarkable friend: able to hear our questions, care about our suffering, and deftly lead us onward." –Sharon Salzberg, author of *Loving Kindness: The Revolutionary Art of Happiness*

"A great service and a sharp challenge: Sylvia Boorstein takes Buddhist teachings from the formal, textual, mnemonic lists where they're kept into the sweating, lusty, angry, ordinary world–where they live or die."
     –David Schneider, co-editor of *Essential Zen* and author of *Street Zen*

"Sylvia Boorstein translates the Buddhist teachings into everyday stories in an amazingly forceful, engaging, and compelling voice. . . . These stories are real and they inspire us, across theoretical differences, to become good human beings, in nonostentatious ways. Sylvia's purity of heart and the truth of her many years of spiritual work . . . shine in this book."
     –Dr. Mary Neill, O.P., University of San Francisco

"A delightful introduction to Buddhist practice and its application to everyday life. Sylvia Boorstein's teachings will be helpful to anyone interested in cultivating wisdom, compassion, and self-awareness."–Frances Vaughan, author of *The Inward Arc*

"With grace and humor Sylvia Boorstein lowers the threshold to enlightenment. She makes the Buddhist inner process affordable for us modern city dwellers. Thus the Buddha becomes our neighbor, the sangha is our neighborhood, and the dharma is just what we are and do. . . . Sylvia's images sneak up on your soul as you find yourself Buddha-ing along with her."   –Zalman M. Schachter-Shalomi

It's Easier Than You Think

It's Easier Than You Think

THE BUDDHIST WAY TO HAPPINESS

Sylvia Boorstein

HarperSanFrancisco

An Imprint of HarperCollins*Publishers*

A TREE CLAUSE BOOK

HarperSanFrancisco and the author, in association with The Basic Foundation, a not-for-profit organization whose primary mission is reforestation, will facilitate the planting of two trees for every one tree used in the manufacture of this book.

HarperCollins Web Site: http://www.harpercollins.com

HarperCollins®, ▲®, HarperSanFrancisco™, and A Tree Clause Book® are trademarks of HarperCollins Publishers Inc.

FIRST EDITION

Library of Congress Cataloging-in-Publication Data:

Boorstein, Sylvia,
It's easier than you think : the Buddhist way to happiness / Sylvia Boorstein. – 1st ed.
p.   cm.
ISBN 0–06–251293–5 (cloth)
ISBN 0–06–251294–3 (pbk.)
1. Religious life–Buddhism.   2. Buddhism–Doctrines.   I. Title
BQ4302.B66   1995
294.3'4448–dc20   95–8046

96 97 98 99 ❖ RRD(H) 10 9 8 7 6

Contents

This book is dedicated to my husband, Seymour,
my lifelong best friend.

•

I am enormously grateful to my friend Martha Ley, who, as a gift
to me, typed and retyped, corrected and encouraged, and said
exactly the right balance of "That's good, Sylvia!" and "You already
said that, Sylvia" to make all the writing a joy. Thank you, Martha.

Jack Kornfield, Joseph Goldstein, and Sharon Salzberg have
been my principal Buddhist teachers. I thank them for their
teaching, for their support, and for their friendship.

All of my students, and particularly my Wednesday morning
Spirit Rock students, have listened to my stories again and again
and again, helping me to hear which ones are useful.

I am grateful to Sharon Lebell for saying, "Sylvia, you have
your own voice," and to Mari Stein, who drew a wonderful
illustration of a talk I gave and said, "Write a book, now!"

I gratefully acknowledge the memory of my parents, Harry and
Gladys Schor, both of whom taught me how to think and how to
laugh.

I

Demystifying Spirituality

Spiritual Is Ordinary

•

A few years ago I was teaching in another city, and the person who was to be my host telephoned me in advance to see if I had any special food requirements. I appreciated his concern and explained my eating preferences. I also mentioned that I don't normally eat much for breakfast but that I do like coffee in the morning. He replied, in a very surprised voice, "You drink *coffee?*" I realized I had just made a heretical confession. I needed to do some fast mind scrambling to find a graceful way to explain to my host (without losing my spiritual stature) that I do, indeed, drink coffee.

There are some peculiar notions about what constitutes "being spiritual." I have a cartoon on the wall of my office that shows two people having dinner in a restaurant. One of them is saying to the other, "It's such a relief to meet someone who isn't on a spiritual quest." I agree. There is an enormous possibility of getting side-tracked into self-conscious holiness, of putting energy into acting the part of a "spiritual person."

A dear friend of mine, as he has become more and more established as a meditation teacher, has become less and less hesitant about telling people he loves football games. He even admits he gets very *excited* about the games, cheering at his television set as if he were sitting in the stadium. No dispassionate attitude of "May the best team win" for him! I know he has a wonderful level of understanding, *and* he behaves like a regular person in a regular world. Being a meditator and developing equanimity do not mean becoming weird.

I think I chose the title for this book long before the book itself was written. Indeed, I was motivated to write largely because I wanted to tell people that spiritual living does not need to be a big deal. Sometimes people decide to make a lifestyle change in the service of waking up. Some people join communities or religious orders. Some people change their diet. Some people become celibate. All of those choices are, for some people, very helpful *tools* for waking up, but they aren't *inherently* spiritual.

Other people choose other tools. In this book, the principal tool, mindfulness, is invisible. Mindfulness, the aware, balanced acceptance of present experience, is at the heart of what the Buddha taught. This book is meant to be a basic Buddhist primer, but no one should be daunted. It's easier than you think.

Managing Gracefully

•

Here's the scene that inspired this book:

I was at a gathering of American Buddhist meditation teachers. At least once a year mindfulness meditation teachers in this country, all friends of mine, meet and spend some days together. We plan our schedules, and we talk about what we're teaching. We also spend a certain amount of time sharing our personal stories. "What's happened to you this year?" "How are things with you?" We take special time to go around the room and share what's going on in our lives.

As I listened to all of us speaking in turn, I was struck by one particular thing. As people spoke, they said things like, "I'm pretty content" or "I'm doing all right" or "I'm pretty happy." And yet, we all told regular stories. People had regular lives with regular Sturm und Drang. People had relationship problems, problems with aging parents; someone's child had a very serious illness; someone else was dealing with a difficult kind of loss. And yet everyone said some variation of "I'm pretty much all right" or "I'm pretty content." And it didn't mean that they weren't struggling with what was happening to them. It did not mean that they had transcended their stories and that they were fine because they felt no pain from them. They *were* struggling and often in quite a lot of pain and concern, but still, they were all right. I thought to myself as I looked around, "What we're all doing is we're all managing gracefully."

Managing gracefully is not second-rate. I'm pleased to think of myself as managing gracefully. It's a whole lot better than ten years ago or twenty years ago when I was managing tensely or fearfully. Everybody manages one way or another; everyone who is alive and reading this book has *managed*. Managing gracefully or even semi-gracefully is terrific.

Enlightenment

•

When I started to practice meditation in the early seventies it was hip. Everybody was meditating; every weekend you could take a workshop in another form of meditation. The advertisements for the workshops usually suggested that at the end of the weekend you'd be totally enlightened.

I remember once going to a party that looked like a regular party—people talking, visiting, and laughing—and in the middle sat a woman with a strange look on her face, eyes closed, face serene, totally tuned out from the whole scene. Somebody leaned over to me and said, "Look at her, she's enlightened," and I thought to myself, "If *that's* what enlightenment is, I don't want it."

What I did want, at least for a while, were exotic powers. I heard extraordinary stories of people who could bilocate or levitate. Sometimes, as I sat on my cushion and experienced an unusual lightness in my body, I imagined I was about to levitate. I hoped I would. I thought it would be a far-out thing, rising up off my cushion and floating in the air.

I think I was also influenced by a story my grandfather told about my grandmother—a woman who died when I was nine years old. I knew her as a sickly old woman, but my grandfather remembered her as the very beautiful woman he had married when she was eighteen years old. He told me she was so beautiful that "she glowed in the dark." I asked him if he really meant that, and he said, "Yes, she really did." He said, "At my nephew Murray Fox's wedding, the hall was lit with gaslight because it was before electricity, so it was quite dark, and everyone said, 'Look at Fischel's wife, she shines in the dark!'" I held that as a wonderful, luminous memory and as an ideal. What I wanted to achieve from my meditation practice was to shine in the dark. I think a lot of us in the early days wanted magic.

My Buddhist meditation teachers, whom I met in 1977, talked about enlightenment but not about magic. They talked about "seeing clearly" and how it could mean happiness and the end of suffering. That sounded like the kind of magic I wanted most.

Waking Up Is Nonsectarian

•

Every religious tradition I know talks about waking up to the truth. Every path I know promises that the direct experience of truth sets us free, brings us peace, compels us to compassionate action in the world. Knowing the truth brings happiness.

Practicing mindfulness and *metta* (lovingkindness) is not religiously challenging. This makes them accessible tools for meditators in all traditions. Awareness, clarity, compassion, generosity, understanding—these are in the middle of *everyone's* spiritual road.

SCENARIO

In my early retreat experience I was part of a large group, perhaps a hundred people, doing intensive mindfulness practice in a monastery in Barre, Massachusetts. Retreats are held in silence, so apart from costume differences, you can't tell who anyone is.

Days passed as we lived and practiced together in silence. I saw Theravadan monks in orange robes, Zen people in traditional Zen clothing, and Tibetan monks and nuns. There were women in rose colored sari-style robes, and I guessed they were part of a Hindu traditional practice. Some people wore red clothes and beads, which meant they were followers of a certain Hindu teacher. One man wore a Franciscan monk habit. I liked passing near him because the long beads and crucifix that hung from his belt made a pleasant clicking sound as he walked.

On Friday evening, I entered the dining room and saw that someone had lit two candles on a small table in the corner of this communal room. Next to the candles was a sign that said, "These are Sabbath candles. Please do not blow them out.

They will burn down by themselves, and I'll remove them tomorrow after sunset."

I looked around and thought, "Here we all are! Our vegetarian diet presents no religious challenges, so everyone can be here. We have a liturgy of silence, so everyone can be here. Each of us, in whatever religious context we live our lives, is trying to wake up. Practicing mindfulness—we can do it together."

The maps in this book are definitely Buddhist maps. They are clear and useful and nonparochial. Truth is truth. Mind-tangles and suffering are universal, and the desire for happiness and the end of suffering is also universal.

2

***

The Path to Happiness

THE BUDDHA'S BASIC TEACHINGS

Basic Wisdom: Mr. Cory and My Grandfather

•

The Buddha's maps for the journey to wisdom and happiness are attractive to many people because they are so simple. Essentially, he taught that it doesn't make sense to upset ourselves about what is beyond our control. We don't get a choice about what hand we are dealt in this life. The only choice we have is our attitude about the cards we hold and the finesse with which we play our hand.

When the Buddha taught his ideas twenty-five hundred years ago, many people understood him so well as soon as they heard him that they were happy ever after. The people who didn't understand him immediately needed to practice meditation, and then they understood.

The Buddha's ideas became the central spiritual teaching for a major part of this planet. His teaching included a vast cosmology, but his essential message about a healthy and happy way to live sounds, to me, like Mr. Cory who lives down the road from me or my grandfather who died ten years ago.

Mr. Cory is ninety years old, and he still farms. He and his wife, the same wife for nearly seventy years, do all the work on their several-acre farm and sell the produce out of their garage. One day last summer I drove down their driveway to buy some onions and saw the garage door open. "Wow!" I thought to myself. "Look what Mr. Cory has done. He's gotten a statue of himself to sit in his open garage door as a decoration." I suppose I had flashed on cigar store wooden Indians of my childhood or life-sized models of Colonel Sanders.

Of course, it wasn't a merchandising gimmick at all. It was Mr. Cory, sitting still as a statue, waiting. He wasn't reading or writing or sorting produce or whittling or doing *anything* but waiting. And it wasn't as if the Corys' produce stand is on a main road where he might be watching the traffic go by. Their garage is behind their house, and their house is on a barely traveled side road. *Nothing* goes by. Mr. Cory didn't have anything he needed to do, so he wasn't doing anything. I never discussed philosophy with Mr. Cory, but my guess is he would say, "If it isn't broken, don't fix it," and "If it is broken, and you can't fix it, don't worry about it."

I stopped my car, got out, and walked all the way to the garage before Mr. Cory moved. Suddenly, I remembered my camera, which I had left in my car, and I said, "Mr. Cory, would it be all right with you if I took your photo?" "Yep," he answered. He never asked, "Why?"

The photo was a good one, a present-day *American Gothic*–Mr. Cory sitting impassively next to crates of tomatoes and zucchini. I framed an enlargement of it and hung it in my office near a photo of Meher Baba, a spiritual teacher I admire. I considered sending the negative to *Country Life* magazine, and I imagined they would print it, giving me photo credit. I framed a copy of the picture and brought it, as a gift, to Mr. Cory. He said, "Thanks."

My grandfather was ninety-eight years old when he died, and he died of oldness. His heart just gave out, but his mind was clear until the end. He had outlived my mother, his oldest daughter, and all three of his wives. He had survived difficult economic times. He had come to America from Europe as a young man, leaving his parents and many sisters and brothers in Austria, never to see any of them again. He worked as a manual laborer because he never learned to read or write. I remember watching him, when I was a little girl, washing his hands after work with a special gritty soap to try to get them clean. He was a passionate, emotional man. When my parents gave birthday parties for me, he would cry when people sang "Happy Birthday."

When my mother died at age forty-seven, my grandfather was seventy-seven years old. Her death was a terrible blow to him, and he was so distraught at her funeral that my principal concern was about how he was going to get through that day. He did not disguise his pain from himself or from anyone else.

My mother died in August, and during summers in those years my grandfather was the maintenance supervisor at a colony of vacation cottages in Maine. A few days after my mother's funeral, my grandfather pulled himself together, emotionally and physically, and went back to work. He said his philosophy-of-life phrase, which I had heard him say many times before: "Well, what can you do?—That's life!" At that time, I thought he was Zorba. He worked many more years, he married again, he enjoyed his great-grandchildren. He remained a good, close friend to my father and was a friend to my father's new wife when my father remarried. He never again visited at the house in which my mother had lived. To go there made him too sad.

I visited my grandfather when he was very, very old, living in a community of elderly folk in south Florida. Twice a day, after breakfast and lunch, he would invite me to accompany him on a walk around the block. It was a long walk, because he walked slowly. He explained to me that this was his regular regimen, his daily exercise. I said to him, "What do you think about when you walk?" He looked at me with surprise. "What do you mean, what do I think about?" he asked. "When I walk, I walk!" By that time, I thought he was the Buddha.

Neither Mr. Cory nor my grandfather ever heard of meditation. I think they paid attention to their lives and became wise. For those of us who don't arrive at wisdom naturally, meditation is one way to get there through practice.

The First Noble Truth: Pain Is Inevitable, Suffering Is Optional

•

The principal map the Buddha used for teaching about the journey to happiness is called the Four Noble Truths.

In the First Noble Truth the Buddha explains that in life "pain is inevitable, but suffering is optional." The Buddha didn't say it in those exact words; he spoke in his vernacular. My rendition in a more current idiom carries the sense of what the Buddha meant to convey and I hope is not irreverent.

Life *is* difficult. Scott Peck said this in the first line of the book *The Road Less Traveled* and sold hundreds of thousands of copies. I sometimes think people read the first sentence and were so excited someone was actually telling the truth of their experience that they bought the book. Life *is* so mysterious. Regardless of our planning, it is essentially unpredictable. For years I had a sign on my bathroom mirror to remind me, daily, that "Life is what happens to you while you are making other plans." All the same, I keep spending time trying to fix up *now* so I'll be happier in the mythical *future*.

I was in my midthirties when I realized with somewhat dramatic alarm that I was totally ill-equipped to deal with how awesome life is. I had somehow managed to keep hidden from myself the tenuous balance in which our happiness hangs from moment to moment. I had grown up and I had done all the things meant to guarantee happiness. I had learned a profession that I was practicing and feeling gratified with; I had gotten married and I had four splendid children whom I loved very much. Somehow, I never thought about how vulnerable it all was, and so I had never thought about any questions of ultimate significance.

One day, down the street from where I lived, two little girls on their way to school were run over and killed by an out-of-control car. They were six and seven years old, and they were sisters. I didn't know them, but I knew about them because they were classmates of my daughter Elizabeth. Suddenly, I woke up to the fact that being alive is very dangerous and every moment of life is very precious. Perhaps if I had woken up to that fact in a balanced way, or at least in a more mature way, I would have experienced one of those transformative moments one reads about, after which one is totally changed forever and the rest of life is lived in abiding clarity. That didn't happen to me. I was plunged into gloom and despair. I couldn't imagine why people continued living if life is terminal at the very best and unpredictable throughout. I realized all relationships end in loss, and loss is so painful. I couldn't figure out why we do it.

The fact that I can write about this period of my life with some lightness now doesn't mean it wasn't a terrible time for me. It was! I read existential philosophers, Camus and Sartre, and I wondered how I had managed to keep this terrible truth hidden from myself all these years. I wondered why everybody else didn't see it. How could people live their lives as if everything were all right, when I absolutely knew it wasn't? I recall teaching psychology students about "existential angst," and I would tell them the Kierkegaard joke: Someone said to Kierkegaard, "I'll see you next Tuesday," and he supposedly responded, "Ha, I'll see you next Tuesday if, as you leave my house, a tile does not fall off the roof and hit you in the head and if, as you cross the street, you are not run over by a carriage out of control," and so forth. It's not a funny joke. I could not say "I'll see you later" to my children as they left for school or even "I hope you have a good time" to anyone without hearing ominous overtones ringing in my ears.

Part of my despair was thinking I was the only person who felt that way. All around me were people who seemed to feel that life was really fine and not worrisome. What a relief it was to me to go to my first meditation retreat and hear people speak the truth so clearly—the First Noble Truth that life is difficult and painful, just by its very nature, not because we're doing it wrong. I was so relieved to meet people who were willing to say life is difficult, often painful, and who still looked fine about admitting it. Most important, they looked *happy*. That was tremendously reassuring to me. I thought to myself, "Here are people who are just like me, who have lives just like mine, who know the truth and are willing to name it and are all right with it."

The Second Noble Truth: Clinging Is Suffering

•

The First Noble Truth declares unflinchingly, straight out, that pain is inherent in life itself just because everything is changing. The Second Noble Truth explains that suffering is what happens when we struggle with whatever our life experience is rather than accepting and opening to our experience with wise and compassionate response. From this point of view, there's a big difference between pain and suffering. Pain is inevitable; lives come with pain. Suffering is not inevitable. If suffering is what happens when we struggle with our experience because of our inability to accept it, then suffering is an optional extra.

I misunderstood this when I started my practice and believed if I meditated hard enough I would be finished with all pain. That turned out to be a big mistake. I was disappointed when I discovered the error and embarrassed that I had been so naive. It's obvious we are not going to finish with pain in this lifetime.

The Buddha said, "Everything dear to us causes pain." I think that's true. I usually don't quote this to beginning students because I don't want them to think of Buddhism as gloomy. But it *is* true. Because things change, our relationship to anything we care about or its relationship to us will change, and we will feel the pain of loss and separation. Those of us who have chosen relational life have made the choice that the pain is worth it.

It is a constant challenge to me (Zen Buddhists might call it a koan) to negotiate the fine line between indifference-to-life-experience and passionate-appreciation-of-life-experience *without* attachment. I'm depending on that being possible, but since every moment has the balance of "pleasant" or "unpleasant," it's hard not to want "pleasant." Fundamentally, it's hard not to want.

St. John of the Cross is said to have prayed, "Lord, spare me visions!" When I began my meditation practice, I wanted visions. It was the late sixties, the Beatles and the Maharishi Mahesh Yogi were popularizing meditation, and the culture was "psychedelic." I wanted something dramatic to happen to me.

Some years later dramatic things *did* happen. During a period of intensive meditation practice, I experienced myself as being filled with light, even radiating light. It was amazing! (In the realm of intensive meditation practice, it's not that big of a deal, but for me, it was amazing.) Quite soon, I began to think it wasn't amazing enough. I began to think about Paul, blinded by the light on the road to Damascus, and since I wasn't blinded, I started to wish for *more* light. I would not have admitted that to anyone, though, because it isn't cool in meditation circles, at least not in mine, to want more rapture—but I did.

The Second Noble Truth of the Buddha is that craving anything *is* suffering. Often it is translated as "the cause of suffering is craving," but I think that misses the point. *Cause* sounds like something happens first and produces a particular result. It could be construed as "crave now, suffer later." I believe it is "crave now, suffer now."

I once heard someone say that a sign of enlightenment was the ability to say (and *mean* it) in any moment, "Well, this isn't what I want, but it's what I got, so okay."

My son Peter's mother-in-law not only tolerates unpleasantness with grace, she often can appreciate it. She is the only person I have ever driven with on Los Angeles freeways, with cars whizzing in and out of lanes arbitrarily, in snarly, congested, smoggy traffic tie-ups, who says, with genuine awe, "Wow! Look at all these people going places!"

It's a big step, of course, from freeways to famines to wars, but it's wonderful to have confirmation that spacious acceptance is humanly possible. Spiritual practice might be discovering that potential in ourselves and enlarging it. The Third Noble Truth says it is indeed possible.

The Third Noble Truth: Terrific Good News

•

A key element of Buddhist spiritual practice is called Right Understanding. One aspect of Right Understanding is clarity about the purpose of mindfulness practice. My entrance into mindfulness practice was totally inspired by Wrong Understanding. I thought if I meditated hard enough I would no longer experience pain. That's wrong, of course. There is no way to be in a body, in a life, without pain.

When I discovered the error of my thinking, I overcame my dismay by inspiring myself with the idea that I could come to the end of *suffering*. That's what the Third Noble Truth is about. It says liberation is possible, peace of mind and happiness—in this very life. It's such an exciting idea!

For some years I taught Eastern religion at a nearby Catholic college. The students were mainly teenagers, graduates of the local Catholic high school. They had, for the most part, lived sheltered and comfortable lives with intact, devout families, in an era between wars. They seemed bewildered when I started to teach Buddhism and introduced, immediately, the idea of suffering. There was no way for me *not* to do that. The notion of suffering and the possible end of suffering is the central teaching of Buddhism. The Buddha himself said this to one particular student. The student, according to the legend, challenged the Buddha. He complained the Buddha had not taught him the cosmology or the philosophy he had hoped he would. The Buddha is said to have replied, "I come to teach only one thing—suffering and the end of suffering."

My young students looked worried when I talked about how, even if things are pleasant, everything is ultimately disappointing because it doesn't last. When I tried the approach of "So often we want things we can't get," they didn't agree. They mostly got the things they wanted. They offered the opinion that Buddhism seemed joyless and then asked, "Do Buddhists have birthday parties?"

I would try hard to find situations of suffering they could relate to. "Did you ever have a girlfriend or boyfriend who stopped liking you? Before you got over it, did it hurt you?"

"Oh," they would say, "if that's what suffering is, I can relate to that!" Even so, I felt a bit dismayed to be the bringer of what seemed to be bad tidings to these young people. I hoped I didn't seem like the Wicked Witch of the West.

I sometimes felt I rushed through the first two Noble Truths to get to the Third Noble Truth, so I could say the glad tidings. It *is* possible to live happily. It *is* possible to cultivate a mind so spacious that it can be passionate and awake and responsive and involved and *care* about things, and not struggle. It is more than good news: it's terrific news.

The Third Patriarch of Zen and the First Patriarch of Berkeley

•

Seng Tsan, the Third Patriarch of Zen, who lived and taught in China in the sixth century, said, "The Great Way is not difficult for those who have no preferences." When I heard that, I thought, "I'll never make it!" Every moment of my experience seemed to present an opportunity to have a preference, and I always did.

At the time I first heard this teaching, my younger daughter was a very serious ballet student, and her teachers thought she was particularly gifted. Every Christmas season she would dance in the ballet company's production of *Nutcracker,* each year graduating into slightly more grown-up roles. Although she was still a child, I would imagine her dancing the Snow Queen someday, and I couldn't believe when that time came it would be all the same to me if she got the part or if someone else's daughter got the part. I had a preference.

I understood the teaching about preferences on the level of trivialities. I knew it would be unlikely I would ever go into a Baskin-Robbins ice cream store and say, "Give me anything," but I also knew I would never be distraught if they were out of chocolate fudge. There are so many almost-as-good possibilities available. This was the level of preferences that translates as personal taste, affinities.

What I could not relate to was that this might be true on the scale of a heart's desire. Indeed, I couldn't figure out why people would *want* to have no preferences. It seemed to me that preferences were what made life fun and exciting. My view was in direct contrast to the teaching of the Diamond Sutra: "Develop a mind that clings to nothing." What I clearly did not understand was that it was possible *and* interesting *and* fun to have hopes and plans and to pursue them with vigor and be prepared to let them go if they didn't work out.

I learned it most dramatically from Bill, a friend of ours who died two decades ago and whom I have come to think of as the First Patriarch of Berkeley. Bill developed cancer while still a young man, in his forties; he had a wife, a flourishing career, and children whom he loved a lot. When he knew his death was approaching, he wrote a letter to all of his friends to be sent after his death. In it, he said about his life, "I would have wanted more, but I never wanted other!" I thought it would be marvelous to live my life that way, wanting more as a response to appreciating life, but never wanting "other."

My friend John Tarrant, a Zen teacher, was telling me about a particular Zen death poem. There are collections of such poems by famous Zen teachers—presumably last-minute insights spoken with their last breaths. John told me one death poem read, "Death poems are all nonsense. Death is just death."

That Zen poet reminds me of my friend Pat, who died of cancer while in her forties, leaving four children, lots of friends, and an interesting law career. From her I learned that you *can* have a preference, a heart's desire preference, not have it come to pass, and not be bitter about it. Pat lived some months after learning her battle with her illness was a losing one. She used that time to reconcile her relationship with her former husband, to finish up all her unfinished law business, and to talk with all her friends and say everything she had wanted to say to them. Some of the things she needed to rectify were emotionally difficult, but she did them anyway. Near the end, she said to me, in quite a conversational, matter-of-fact way, "You know, I've really grown a lot emotionally from this cancer. I've done things I would not have done if I hadn't had it. But, honestly, I would rather not have had it and not grown."

Plain truth. Growing is not that great. Living is better. Given what she couldn't change, she lived her last days with grace. The day before she died, I found her sitting up in bed reading the newspaper. "I've done everything else," she said, "now I'm just waiting." I think that qualifies Pat as the First Matriarch of San Anselmo.

Emily never got to be the Snow Queen. It didn't work out for her to be a dancer, and her grace about it allowed me to let go of my expectations. I still love watching *Nutcracker,* and I particularly enjoy imagining what the Snow Queen's mother must be feeling. I feel much the same when I watch a football game on television and see how the camera pans, immediately after a great end-zone catch, to the player's mother applauding in the stands. I am so touched, I often cry. I also cry when I see sad things happen to people. Meditation doesn't cure crying. I'm glad it doesn't.

The Third-and-a-Half Noble Truth

•

The Buddha taught that the end of suffering was possible. We could, he taught, condition the mind to such spacious clarity that our experience would come and go in a great sea of wise and spacious mind. Pain and joy would come and go, being pleased and being disappointed would come and go, and the mind would remain essentially tranquil. It's incredibly freeing to know you don't need to be pleased in order to be happy.

However, the end of suffering hasn't happened for me yet. It's not from lack of right aspiration. I aspire! Nor is it from not understanding. I believe with all my heart that freedom is possible. I know the tendency to struggle in the mind comes from taking one's own story personally rather than seeing it as part of the great unfolding cosmic drama. I know for *sure* everything is conditioned, and I more or less believe in karma. Nevertheless, I struggle and I suffer. I suffer less than I used to, though, and I'm not as distraught about the suffering as I used to be.

So, I have added an extra half Noble Truth. The half-extra truth is: "Suffering is manageable." Short of coming to the very end of suffering, which I absolutely have faith in as a possibility, I am content with managing my suffering better. Since I know suffering is manageable, I am not as frightened of pain as I used to be. These days I often tell new students right away that although the Buddha taught the end of suffering was possible, I myself am not there yet. They are not dismayed. Nor do I seem to lose any credibility. It's great news for them to hear that suffering is manageable.

That extra half of a Noble Truth also keeps me more compassionate toward myself and toward others. I can see how I get trapped in my stories, how I struggle, how I suffer, how I wish I didn't, and how ultimately things change and resolve. I am kinder to myself when I see how much pain I storm up in my mind through its own conditioned clingings. Acknowledging my own suffering, in spite of the years of practice and whatever wisdom or understanding I might have, makes me sensitive to what must be the *enormous* pain of all the people I'm sharing this planet with.

My Heart Still Clings

•

In a love song, the line "My heart clings to you" would be a desirable sentiment. We want our lover's heart and thoughts to cling to us. In Buddhist understanding, clinging is the cause of suffering. Nevertheless, my heart still clings. On better days, it clings less than it used to.

One of the things I most enjoyed about my early days of meditation practice was listening to stories about the Buddha and his teachings. Long before I had any sense of being able to calm the mind or any sense of what freedom was about, I loved hearing stories about the possibility of freedom.

The early Buddha stories are miraculous. Usually a story begins with a description of the particular place the Buddha was teaching and names the main people who came to listen to him. Usually the stories say, "So-and-so rendered homage to the Buddha and then sat down to hear the discourse." They continue, "And the Blessed One spoke the following words," and then they present a sermon in which the Buddha described the nature of how things are. The stories usually end with the words "As So-and-so listened, he became entirely enlightened" or "As the assemblage listened, they all became entirely enlightened." It is usually phrased this way: "And their hearts, through not clinging, were liberated from taints." I love that. For all the many years of my practice, continuing into the present, whenever I am about to hear someone deliver a discourse, I imagine that this could be the time for my own total and final liberation. The fact that it happened in the days of the Buddha suggests there's a good precedent. It just hasn't happened, yet, to me.

One way of understanding why it doesn't happen easily is to think of the mind as conditioned to certain habitual ways of responding. Mind habits are hard to change. I used to have the habit of getting a headache whenever I felt angry, because I didn't know how to comfortably express displeasure. I am much more comfortable now about expressing angry feelings, but sometimes I need to have a headache to remind myself I'm angry. Also, I am totally convinced that suffering arises when I struggle with events in my life that I cannot change; yet, from time to time, I persist in the struggle. Habits die hard.

I have a theory about why psychological and spiritual mind habits are hard to completely erase. Let's call it the T-shirt theory of mind change. A long time ago, a television commercial showed a mother holding up a T-shirt that her son had worn, indicating the places where he had soiled it with peanut butter and jelly, where he had dropped his chocolate ice cream, and where he had been rolling on the ground playing football. She placed the T-shirt in the washing machine with a particular detergent that the viewer was urged to buy. When she took it out, there was no smudge on it at all, and it looked completely new. In my lifetime of laundry experience, I have never seen a T-shirt come out of the washing machine looking entirely new. There is always some residual discoloration, and even on those rare occasions when all the soil is washed out, the T-shirt itself never hangs exactly as straight as it did when it was brand new. Signs that the shirt has been worn before cling to it forever. I think it's the same with minds, and I think that's okay. If we know which side of the shirt is shorter, we can tuck it in tighter on that side, and it will look perfectly presentable.

If my mind didn't cling, I would be totally fearless. Nothing would frighten me, because there would be nothing I would be afraid to lose and nothing I would need to be happy. But my mind still does cling, so I am sometimes frightened that I won't have what I think I need or that I'll lose what I think I want. It's not such a big problem anymore because fear doesn't frighten me as much as it used to. I know it's from clinging, and I know it will pass. I can tell myself, "I'm frightened now because even though I know what's true, I have forgotten it right now. I know the possibility of remembering exists." That possibility, that conviction, gives me a lot of hope in the middle of the biggest fright.

The Fourth Noble Truth:
The Eightfold Circle

•

Suppose we use a traveling metaphor for the universal spiritual quest. The main map the Buddha offered for the trip to happiness and contentment is called the Eightfold Path, but I have often thought it should be called the Eightfold Circle. A path goes from here to there, and the nearer you are to *there*, the farther you are from *here*. A path is progressive, like a ladder, and, just as you cannot suddenly leap onto the fifth rung of a ladder and start climbing, on a genuine path you would need to start at the beginning and proceed in a linear way until the end. With a circle, you can join in anywhere, and it's the same circle.

When the Buddha taught his path, he said it had a specific number of constituent parts; people could be sure they were going the right way if they saw any one of eight special markers. These signposts are: Right Understanding, Right Aspiration, Right Action, Right Speech, Right Livelihood, Right Effort, Right Concentration, and Right Mindfulness. Travelers seeing any of the signposts will know they are headed in the direction of happiness.

The order in which the traveler sees the signs doesn't matter. If we look at any sign closely, it becomes apparent that each one has all of the others hidden inside it. Even a tiny bit of Right Understanding, the *suspicion* that it is possible to be contented even when we aren't pleased, arouses Right Aspiration to make a lot of Right Effort to develop more Right Understanding. Anyone who decides to practice Right Speech, making sure every single thing she says is both truthful and helpful, discovers it cannot be done without Right Mindfulness. Right Mindfulness means paying attention in every moment, and those who do that soon discover they have Right Concentration as well. Even if a person said, "Eightfold is too complicated. I just want to do a onefold practice," it wouldn't work. It's all connected.

On the journey to happiness, you start anywhere. You start wherever you are. I have only one hesitation about calling the practice a circle. Even a small circle takes up space, and space creates the idea of a *here* and a *there*. There isn't any *there*. When we wake up to happiness, we get to be more *here* than we ever were before. But, since waking up does happen and practice does work, we need to call it something. I guess it's more like the Eightfold Dot.

Right Understanding:
My Friend Alta and "The Change"

•

Whenever people talk about the Buddha's formula for happiness, they start by talking about Right Understanding. Right Understanding means believing, at least a little bit, that even though life is *inevitably* disappointing, it is still possible to be happy. Many people are immediately interested in the idea that there is first aid for life's sadnesses but are reluctant to think about the *inevitability* part. The inevitability part is what is liberating, though, because without it we think that things would have turned out permanently perfect if we had just been more clever or tried a little harder. Nothing turns out permanently perfect, because nothing is permanent.

Awareness of impermanence is a crucial component of wisdom, and although the Buddha taught many things, he taught about impermanence literally with his dying breath. It was the next-to-last sentence he is reported to have said before he died: "Transient are all conditioned things." That means, "Everything changes."

My friend Alta was seventy-nine years old when she died. I met her twenty-five years earlier when she signed up for a yoga class I was teaching. She told me, "My husband has just died after being sick a very long time, and I'm starting to build my life over again." She became interested in consciousness classes and took every course I ever taught. She may have thought of me as her teacher, but, in fact, she was mine.

The paradigmatic Alta story happened ten years ago. She strained her back, probably during her daily three-mile jog, and, because her pain was severe, her friends convinced her to consult a doctor.

"When was the last time you had a complete physical?" asked Dr. S.

"Thirty-five years ago," was Alta's response.

Dr. S's eyebrows shot up. "Thirty-five *years?* How about your breast exams and mammograms?"

"I never had any."

"How about 'the change'?" he asked.

"I went through it," Alta replied.

Going through changes was what Alta was very good at, and, in that ability, she was my role model. We became good friends and spent many rainy winter days in her sewing room making clothing, usually for me. I would talk about my family, and she would talk about hers—the kind of conversations women have when they sew together. I was often relieved to see that what I was fretting over as a problem didn't appear to her to be a big deal, and I noticed she could tell me about a difficulty in her family that seemed to me to be *huge* while she kept right on sewing, not missing a stitch. I knew she was sad, but she appeared at ease. "Aren't you upset?" I would ask. "I've done all I could about it," she would say, "so there is no point in being upset."

Once we really get it that everything changes, we can have a wiser relationship to the events of our lives. If things are painful and we cannot change them, we can, at least, be confident that our pain will not last forever. Often, it is the *thought* that pain will never end that makes it seem unbearable. People trying to console friends who have suffered a bereavement say things like, "Time will heal this," but it's hard for the hearer to believe. In the moment, it doesn't feel like it's true. Right Understanding means feeling terrible, remembering pain is finite, and taking some solace from that remembering. And, when things are pleasant, even splendidly pleasant, remembering impermanence doesn't diminish the experience—it enhances it.

Right Aspiration: Practicing Being Different

•

Many, many years ago, when I was in my early twenties and flying in an airplane was still a novelty to me, I flew to New York City from Atlanta, Georgia. It was a rainy day, and the propeller plane didn't fly above the weather so we bounced around a lot. I gripped the arms of my seat, clenched my teeth, took my pulse a lot, and counted the minutes until landing. The "older woman" in the seat next to me (a woman probably my current age) sat impassively, accepted the flight attendant's offer of lunch, and ate it. "How come she isn't frightened?" I thought to myself. When we touched down on the runway in New York, I whispered, "Thank God!" She turned to me and smiled. "You said it!" she replied. What a piece of news that was to me. She had been frightened, too, but she had eaten her lunch.

My friend Elizabeth had a mastectomy ten years ago, and as her husband, Jim, and I waited outside the recovery room, the nurses came by to give us progress reports and to tell us how cheerful Elizabeth had been on the way to surgery. They marveled at how relaxed she had seemed, how fearless. I later told Elizabeth what the nurses had said. "Were you really not frightened at all?" I asked. She laughed and said, "I was *terrified,* but I didn't think there was any point in making everyone uncomfortable."

Neither the woman on the plane nor my friend Elizabeth was in denial about her feelings. Neither of them was pleased with what was going on, but neither of them had a choice about it. The only choice they had was the style they selected for passing the time. Having the ability to choose a style seems to me to be a great liberation. Perhaps it is the ultimate meaning of "freedom of choice."

Right Aspiration is what develops in the mind once we understand that freedom of choice is possible. Life is going to unfold however it does: pleasant or unpleasant, disappointing or thrilling, expected or unexpected, all of the above! What a relief it would be to know that whatever wave comes along, we can ride it out with grace. If we got really good at it, we could be like surfers, delighting especially in the most complicated waves.

What Right Aspiration translates to in terms of daily action is the resolve to behave in a way that stretches the limits of conditioned response. If I want to build big biceps, I need to use every opportunity to practice lifting weights. If I want to live in a way that is loving and generous and fearless, then I need to practice overcoming any tendency to be angry or greedy or confused. Life is a terrific gym. Every situation is an opportunity to practice. In formal Buddhist language, this is called the cultivation of nonhatred, nongreed, and nondelusion.

Ronna's Grandmother

•

Ronna's grandmother practiced anger. During the last thirty years of her life, she carried on a nonspeaking feud with Ronna's mother. The feud continued even as her memory dimmed. One day, very near her death, the old woman asked Ronna, "Do you recall what I am angry at your mother about?" Ronna *did* recall, but she decided it wouldn't be helpful to bring it up again. "No," she said, "I don't remember." "Neither do I," said the grandmother, "but I remember that I am angry."

Exercising the anger muscle so much that it operates on automatic pilot seems so sad to me. I am most dismayed when I hear someone say, "I'm never going to forgive So-and-so as long as I live!" I think to myself, "What a terrible choice this person is making. She has already been hurt by this other person, and now she is planning to continue the hurt long after the event by enshrining it in memory." The image that often comes to mind is from cowboy movies of the 1940s, where a sheriff puts a rowdy person in a jail cell and shuts the door but doesn't lock it. The joke is that the prisoner shouts and rattles the bars of the cell while the audience knows he needs only to turn the handle in order to get out.

Sometimes it seems to me we go even one step beyond rattling the bars. Instead of rescuing ourselves, we maintain our position of righteous indignation by recounting our grievances. It is the equivalent of having the key to the cell in our hand, reaching around and locking ourselves in, and then throwing the key across the room.

In a famous sermon in the Jetavana Grove, the Buddha taught that people who continue to think about how they have been abused or embarrassed will never be released from their hatred. People who can abandon those thoughts, he continued, are able to be loving. I was explaining this to a class one day, when a student burst out, "Of *course,* that's true, Sylvia. Forgiveness is the price you have to pay for freedom." "Tom," I said, "that's a great line. Can I use it to teach with?" He replied, "Sure, but you must always say, 'Tom said it.'" I always have.

Mary Kay and the Onions

•

You never know when, or over what, an attack of greed can break out. Right Aspiration is the attempt to head off such attacks at the pass. My good friend Mary Kay and I were planting onions last fall, exactly on the full moon in October. The almanac says the full moon ensures the largest crop. It is slow work because each delicate onion shoot needs to be planted individually, but it is also very pleasant because the weather is cool and we have time to talk with each other.

We were congratulating ourselves on managing to plant on the particularly auspicious day, and I said, "What if we have a really *enormous* crop? Do you suppose the onions will keep if we store them under the house? Would we have to dry them? Do people chop them up and put them in baggies in the freezer?" "We could always give them to the soup kitchen," Mary Kay said, "or the homeless shelter." Mary Kay is the director of a homeless shelter, and I often bring things there. However, in that moment I knew that, although I was prepared to go to the market and buy a truckload of onions for the shelter, I wanted the onions from *this* garden to go into *my* stomach. An onion is an onion, and I was planting because I enjoy planting, not because I cannot buy an onion, and yet here I was feeling the pang of a hypothetical future loss. It is real pain, the grasping of the mind over what it thinks it needs—even if it's just an onion. I avoided the possible additional suffering of confessing to my greed by getting over it. "Of course we will," I said, and I meant it. It was a great relief.

In the Jimtown store in the Alexander Valley in California where I live, there is a sign that says, "Liberty is not license to do whatever you want to do. It is the freedom to do what you ought to do."

Collin and the Convent

•

I made a vow to myself, some years ago, that if something was frightening to me and yet within the realm of what I could reasonably expect of myself, I would do it. My general guideline, "If other people do it, I can do it," propelled me to do some things that would otherwise have seemed daunting to me. The vow allowed me to scuba dive and see the amazing underwater world, and it sustained me through intense and extraordinary meditation experiences for a close-up look at the amazing inner world.

Fearfulness is a mind habit. Some people have it more than others. It is always extra. Being trapped by fear is a form of delusion. Either I can do something or I can't. If I truly can't—I am mechanically inept, so piloting a plane would be unwise—I don't do it. If I truly can, and it would be a wholesome thing to do, I push myself. I figured out one day that fear is a series of neuronal discharges in the brain, and I resented feeling I was being held captive by cerebral squiggles.

Grandmothers often have the role of spiritual teacher. My grandmother was my first teacher, and I hope I am carrying on in her tradition. The lesson I learned best from her was fortitude in the face of disagreeable situations. "Where is it written," she would ask, "that you are supposed to be happy all the time?"

I took my grandson Collin to visit my friend Mary when he was three years old. Mary is a member of the Dominican Sisters of San Rafael and at the time of our visit was living in a wonderful, huge convent that had for many years served as the mother house of her order. It had tall, heavy, imposing doors and a very long staircase leading up to them. Mary had spoken to me about how formidable passing through those big doors had been for her thirty years earlier when she had entered as a novice. Collin didn't like the entrance either.

"I don't like these steps, Grandma. Let's go home."

"Now is not going-home time. Now is visiting–Aunt Mary time."

"I *really* don't like these steps, Grandma."

"You don't have to like them, Collin. You just have to go up them. Hold my hand, and we'll do it together."

We paid our visit, of course, and Collin enjoyed himself. He came out a Master of Long Staircases. "Wow, look at those stairs, Grandma!" He felt good about his triumph, and I felt good about beginning his spiritual training. I tell the story of Collin often to students, especially those doing meditation in a retreat setting. I tell it when people say, "I'm experiencing myself and my mind in a new way, so I'm frightened." I want them to know that new and unfamiliar often feels frightening, but it doesn't need to. If someone holds our hand, "frightened" changes to "interested," and "interested" is one of the Factors of Enlightenment.

Right Action

•

Codes of ethics are most often associated with prohibitions: Don't do this, don't do that. All the spiritual traditions I know have more or less the same list of don'ts. This makes sense, since all the don'ts elaborate on the awareness that if we are not alert, our naturally arising impulses of greed and anger might lead us to do something exploitive or abusive. The fundamental rule is, "Don't cause pain."

Traditional Buddhist texts, when they talk about Right Action, use the terms *hiri* and *ottappa*, usually translated as "moral shame" and "moral dread." Shame and dread have ominous overtones in English, but I rather like these terms. I appreciate the sense of awesome responsibility they are meant to convey. Collectively, what they mean is that every single act we do has the *potential* of causing pain, and every single thing we do has consequences that echo way beyond what we can imagine. It doesn't mean we shouldn't act. It means we should act carefully. Everything matters.

My Grandfather and the Oranges

•

I can't remember not knowing about my grandfather and the oranges, but I guess I must have heard the story from him when I was nine or ten years old. I was probably asking him why, since he worked as a gas station attendant, he didn't know how to drive a car.

"When I came to America," he said, "I was twenty-five years old, and someone tried to teach me to ride a bicycle. I wasn't so steady about it, and one day I accidentally bumped into a woman carrying bags of groceries. One bag fell on the ground, and oranges rolled all over the street. I was so upset at the trouble I had caused, I never wanted to drive anything again!"

"But that was just one time," I protested.

"It doesn't matter," he replied. "Once I saw what it was to bump into someone, I never wanted to bump into anyone again."

Perhaps that was an extreme level of *hiri* and *ottappa*, but I admired my grandfather a lot. And, over the years as I heard the story frequently repeated, I felt my grandfather was pleased with his decision. He lived out his desire not to hurt anyone. As he expressed it in his own form of English, "I never wanted to cause nobody no trouble."

Affirmative Right Action:
Airplane First Aid

•

Behavioral prohibitions are only half of Right Action. The other half is taking every opportunity to alleviate pain. Adopting the whole world is much more than a noble gesture on behalf of others: it's a fine thing to do for oneself.

I have sometimes felt, retrospectively, very sad about having passed up an opportunity to act in a way that might have relieved some suffering. I missed a chance five years ago, on an airplane, and I have remembered it and taught about it a lot since then. Last week I almost missed another opportunity, on another airplane, but I caught myself just in time. Afterward, I wondered whether my first mistake had been erased by my current correction, and I decided that kind of thinking is irrelevant. Right action is a permanent call. There is no balance point, where we've evened the score. If action is required and wholesome action can be taken, it needs to be taken. This sounds like a big job, like the bodhisattva vow to end all suffering, and it is. It's not a *hard* job, though. Decisions get easier. Since sloughing off is not an option, the only task is figuring out what's wholesome and doing it.

Airplane First Aid I: The Mistake

•

I was in my seat, buckled in, as the last passengers boarded the Boston–San Francisco flight. It was the irritated sound of the mother's voice that first caught my attention. I looked up and saw that her face was flushed and strained. Her young son looked pale and frightened. She was juggling carry-on bags, shoving the little boy ahead of her toward their seats, scolding him at every step. I winced, I thought bad thoughts about her, and I looked the other way.

It was a six-hour flight. The mother and son sat a few rows behind me, and, periodically, I could overhear her speaking harshly. Each time I heard her, I felt upset. I wished I were on another plane. I felt annoyed at the woman for messing up what I had hoped would be a relaxing flight for me. I worried about the boy and constructed various grim scenarios for how his life would turn out. I thought about how, someday, this woman's action would surely haunt her. I did everything but help.

At the time, no solution for intervention occurred to me. Perhaps I felt so upset I thought I would blurt out something unkind. Maybe I was afraid she would react angrily. "What could I say," I asked myself, "that would be helpful?"

The plane landed, and the woman and her son disappeared into the crowd. Then, perhaps because my flood of judgments stopped, I knew what I could have done. I could have stopped at her seat, smiled, and said, "It's very hard traveling alone with a child, isn't it? I did it, too, long ago, and I remember. How long have you been traveling? Did you need to wait long in the airport? Where are you going? Will someone meet you?" Not *all* of those questions, of course. Any one or two of them would have let her know I had noticed her distress and cared enough to ask. That would have helped.

Who knows what might have happened if she and I had talked? Maybe I could have told her something useful about child raising. Maybe I could have interested her in trying to change. Maybe that little boy's life would have been different.

The things I *might* have done seemed very clear afterward, when it was too late to do them. I felt remorse. Buddhists talk about actions "conditioning" other actions, and my non-action conditioned a determination to do better.

Airplane First Aid II: The Correction

•

Five years later, once again settled in my seat on United flight 33, Boston–San Francisco, I was looking forward to six hours of writing time, since I was only weeks away from the manuscript due date for this book. The woman next to me seemed clearly uncomfortable, fidgeting in her seat, eager to engage in conversation. She told me she bruised her coccyx in a recent fall and sitting was painful for her. She explained she was worried because the flight would be too long for her to be comfortable without smoking a cigarette.

I allowed some time for conversation, hoping she would settle down so I could write without seeming impolite. I shuffled my papers in a way that suggested I wanted to work. Each time we concluded a topic and I began to turn away, she started in on a new subject.

Lunch came and went. I had hoped our mealtime conversation would allow me to resume writing in earnest, but that didn't happen. The longer the flight wore on, the more uncomfortable she became. Her back hurt and she missed smoking.

It was actually she, and not I, who caught me before I had made a mistake. We had mentioned our respective jobs, and she asked a long string of questions about what I did as a meditation teacher: Whom did I teach? Was what I taught good for people with stress? Was it hard to learn? How could she learn? Eagerly, she had me write down names of books she could read, tapes she could buy, places she might go to study.

Finally, I got it. I said, "Would you like me to teach you to meditate right now? It might make you feel better."

"Yes, I would," she said. "I really would."

I put down the writing. I gave some meditation instructions. She sat quietly for a while. Then we talked about her experience.

She said she felt more relaxed. We talked about how feeling a *little* better made her feel *much* better, because now she was sure she would survive the trip. We talked about how the mind takes pain and blows it up bigger than it really is.

I began to realize I was having a good time. It occurred to me that it was totally ludicrous to be writing a book about the joys of selfless acts of kindness, about relating with compassion every chance we get, while trying to ignore a person in pain sitting next to me. During the last half hour of the flight she fell asleep, and I wrote something really good.

Right Speech: When You Give Someone Your Word, It Might Be Forever

•

A sign in the Jimtown store near my home says:

> Be careful of the words you use,
> Keep them short and sweet,
> You never know from day to day
> Which ones you'll have to eat.

I think a lot about the fact that the Buddha made a separate category for Right Speech. He could have been more efficient and included it in Right Action, since speaking is a form of action. For a while I thought it was separate because we speak so much. But then I changed my mind—some people *don't* speak a lot. Now, I think it's a separate category because speech is so potent.

I read a sentence in a magazine years ago, a page filler added to the bottom of a column because the article wasn't quite long enough. I don't recall what magazine it was or what the article was about, but I remember the sentence. It said, "Sticks and stones may break my bones, but words can always harm me."

Sometimes, in a class, I will say, "Raise your hand if you have ever broken a bone." After people raise their hands, I say, "Leave your hand up if that bone still hurts you now." Usually, all the hands come down. Then I say, "Raise your hand if you still feel pain from something someone said to you in the past year." Lots of hands go up. "Keep your hand up if you have pain from a remark someone made about you in the last five years." Hands stay up. "Last ten years . . . twenty years . . . thirty years . . . a remark made before you were five years old." Many people still have an arm in the air. They look around at each other and smile, sheepishly, but I don't think anyone is amused. It is a lovely moment of shared compassion, of being a witness to the burden we have all borne of carrying the pain of hurtful remarks. Perhaps we think that if we are mature adults we should have gotten over the rebukes of childhood. I wonder if we ever do. I think we are all quite vulnerable, like cream puffs, crisp on the outside but fragile inside and very sweet.

During the 1960s, when the social ethos was "letting it all hang out," I had recurrent fantasies about writing a book called *Holding It All In*. I think I was alarmed that people had overlooked how vulnerable each of us is. In recent years, I've revised my book title to *Holding It All In Until We've Figured Out How to Say It in a Useful Way*.

I believe we are obliged to tell the truth. Telling the truth is a way we take care of people. The Buddha taught complete honesty, with the extra instruction that everything a person says should be truthful *and* helpful.

When the Buddha taught Right Speech, he provided a guide for making corrections. Admonitions, he said, should be timely, truthful, gentle, kind, and helpful. When I tell people those criteria, they often exclaim, "But then no one could ever admonish anyone!" I think otherwise. I think with Right Speech people can make suggestions or observations in a way that the other person can hear and use them without feeling diminished.

Advanced Right Speech Exercises:
Is What I Am About to Say an
Improvement over Maintaining Silence?

•

Entry-level Right Speech is speech that doesn't add pain to any situation. This takes care of the obvious mistakes, like telling lies or purposely using speech hurtfully. High-level Right Speech maintains the balance of situations by not adding the destabilizing element of gossip.

Gossiping is talking about someone not present. Except on rare occasions when one might need to convey a need on behalf of another person, gossip is extra. Talking disparagingly about a third person is inviting the listener to share your grumbly mind space. Talking admiringly about a third person might cause your listener to feel unimportant. Why not choose to talk about current experience?

Here is an exercise in advanced Right Speech. Starting tomorrow when you wake up, don't gossip. See what happens if you just give up making comments about anyone not present. Listen carefully to the voice in your mind as it is getting ready to make a comment, and think to yourself, "Why am I saying this?" Awareness of intention is the best clue for knowing whether the remark you are about to make is Right Speech. Is your intention wholesome, a desire to help? Or to show off? Or to denigrate?

Sometimes gossip seems neutral, an attempt to make conversation, to fill the space radio announcers call "empty air." I think we do this out of concern that our companions will think we are not interested enough in them to talk to them. It's a pleasure to be able to be with someone and say, "I am having a wonderful time and am enjoying walking with you (eating with you, listening to music with you, gathering seashells with you), so we don't need to talk." I come from a long line of champion talkers, so it was a surprise to me to find how much I enjoyed the silence of meditation retreats where there is no talking at all. Making a salad, silently, with someone is very companionable. Indeed, sharing silent salad-making space with a stranger for a week arouses a sense of being intimate friends.

Very high level Right Speech requires awareness of intention in *all* communication, not just gossip. I began tidying up my own speech after a period of silent retreat practice. When I returned home, it was several days before my speech returned to its accustomed reflexive speed. I was able to notice that in the interim between answers arising in my mind and emerging from my mouth, I had enough time to become aware of my motivation. My motivation turned out to be pretty good but not as good as I had imagined. Maybe 80 percent of my answers were fact disclosure, 10 percent of the time I was motivated by pleasure over the clever way I was going to say them, and 10 percent of the time I was trying to bias the listener's understanding. Sometimes it was even worse! Sometimes the final 10 percent was a covert dig, an underhanded way to get even for some real (or imagined) slight.

Initially, I was dismayed to find I was using my gift for verbal nuance as a way of being secretly unkind, but I felt better as soon as I decided not to do it anymore. High-level Right Speech turns out not to be very difficult. Once the mind is programmed to scan for hidden messages, it does it automatically. Making the change has simplified my life, since I have much less cleaning up to do afterward.

Ultimate high level Right Speech is truthfulness to the *n*th degree, which requires impeccability of presence. I learned about it from Jim, a psychologist whom I met when we were teaching together at a Buddhist-Christian dialogue conference. I had read his books and was glad to go to dinner with him.

"What do you think of topic A, Sylvia?" he asked. (I use generic topics because I don't recall what we talked about, and what I learned from Jim had more to do with *how* we talked than with any topic.)

"I think this, this, and this," I responded immediately. "What do you think about topics B and C?"

He just sat there. "Oh, dear, " I thought. "Perhaps I've offended him. Maybe those topics were too personal. Maybe too many topics."

By and by he said, "What I think about B and C is this and this. What do you think about D?"

"Oh, D," I said, "I think this, this, and this. How about E and F?"

Again he sat quietly. I was beginning to wake up to what was happening. When I asked him what he *thought*, he took time to *think*. He was responding by telling me what he thought now, not yesterday or last week. I felt complimented. I felt he respected my questions enough to tell me his most current truth about it.

The exercise for ultimate high level Right Speech is the Sixty Second Rule for conversation. Any time a person asks a question, the respondent needs to pause sixty seconds before answering. Since the pause is obligatory, the likelihood is that the answer will include reflection, examination of intention, preview of tone—all the things that make for a wise response.

Right Livelihood: Pearl and the Ironing

•

Right Livelihood appears to be harder to practice these days than in the time of the Buddha. The rule is still the same: Right Livelihood is organizing one's financial support so that it is nonabusive, nonexploitive, nonharming. However, these days what is abusive and exploitive is not necessarily self-evident.

When the Buddha taught, unwholesome livelihood categories were easy to distinguish. Soldiering, keeping slaves, manufacturing weapons and intoxicants—all were on the proscribed list. In our time, soldiers sometimes serve as peacekeepers. It's hard to know the wholesomeness of all the products of any corporation, corporate mergers being what they are. Who knows what else is being manufactured by my detergent company's subsidiaries?

"So-and-so is a very successful person" often means "So-and-so has accumulated a lot of money." It doesn't necessarily mean So-and-so is ethical or moral or happy. The Buddha's teachings on Right Livelihood didn't preclude affluence—he taught everyone, including kings—but it wasn't based on wealth. It was based on *wholesomeness*.

For me, a complete picture of wholesome Right Livelihood is even larger than the proscriptions that reflect *external* choices. Wholesome *internal* choices—healthy attitudes about one's work—also contribute to mental happiness and peace of mind. Everyone's livelihood is an opportunity for self-esteem.

My friend Pearl began working as our housekeeper when my four children were very young and I was starting graduate school. I was proud of myself for having been accepted at a prestigious school, and Pearl was happy with her new job.

Pearl was a good cook, in the hearty, Midwestern style my children loved. She drove carpools, remembered dentist appointments, and ministered to sick children. One evening, after a day at school,

I returned home and found her finishing a week's worth of ironing. The ironing was hanging on an ironing tree, an item very few people own any more.

"Pearl," I exclaimed, "that ironing looks wonderful!"

"It does," she replied. "I really pride myself on my ironing."

I'm glad I was awake to Pearl's response. I remember it today, thirty-some years later. It wasn't that I had an uppity attitude about professional work; I didn't. What I learned from Pearl in that moment was that *what* you do, externally, is only half of the story. What it does for you, internally, is the other half!

Right Effort: "Remember, Be Happy"

•

Traditional instructions for Right Effort are straightforward. The Buddha used the special terms *wholesome* and *unwholesome* to mean that which leads to happiness and that which leads to unhappiness. The guidelines are: Notice when wholesome feelings such as friendliness, compassion, or generosity are present in the mind, and encourage them to grow. Practice acting on those feelings as a way of generating happiness. Notice, as well, when unwholesome feelings like anger and greed arise in the mind, and try not to encourage them to grow. Furthermore, the instructions suggest that such unwholesome feelings be put out of the mind.

I believe the Buddha meant we have a choice about mind states. This is easier said than done. Greed and anger, at least in little bursts, have a rousing energetic effect, and they are seductive. Perhaps that's why he called it Right Effort and Right Choice. Once, many years ago, I drove to the Oakland Airport in the middle of the night to meet my husband, who was arriving home on a late flight. The deserted freeway was monotonous. I began to feel drowsy, and then I felt alarmed that I would fall asleep at the wheel. Suddenly, in the passing flow of my thoughts, I remembered a problem I was having with a distant relative and felt annoyance over what that person presumably had said about me.

"Some nerve, she has!" I thought, and in that moment I felt myself awake. A hit of righteous indignation had banished the drowsiness.

"Wow, this is great!" I congratulated myself on my new discovery. "Mind states are interchangeable. I can replace one with another. I can wake myself by thinking angry thoughts."

And I did. All the way to the airport, I thought angry thoughts and replayed different dialogues: what I said, what she said I said, what I could tell everyone about what she said I said. By the time I pulled into the airport parking lot, I was wide awake. I don't remember for certain, but my guess is I was probably a bit feisty and irritable as well—not the best mind states for a homecoming reunion.

Two days later, I recounted the whole driving episode to my teacher, assuming he would congratulate me on my new insight into the mind and body relationship. He laughed and said, "Sure, it's true about replacing mind states. However," he added, "you could have woken yourself up with a sexy thought as well, and that would have been more fun." It probably would also have put me in a better mood for a homecoming.

Much later I began to appreciate that apart from the little bursts of greed and anger, which are the natural responses of the mind to pleasant and unpleasant experiences, lingering in either valence is tedious. Prolonged yearning and prolonged aversion are both tiring and demoralizing. They fatigue the mind. That's another reason they are hard to dispel. I think we get too tired to climb out of them or see through them. We need guidelines to remind us. Sometimes we need people to remind us.

I was driving across the Golden Gate Bridge on my way to meet a friend for an evening at the opera with my mind filled, for whatever reason, with a grumpy mood. I missed the entire panorama of the bay wrapping around San Francisco with its evening lights coming on, I cruised into the toll gate, and I handed my commute ticket to the toll taker. "Have a *really* terrific evening," he said. Zap! A thrill of alertness went through me. "What on earth have I been doing?" I thought. "Here I am, meeting a friend I love, to do an activity I love, and I'm brooding."

Unquestionably, there are sad things in the world right now, even in my life right now, but grumbling doesn't make anything better. In fact, it makes things worse. The Buddha taught, "Every mind moment conditions the next." Grumbling gets the mind bogged down in the weariness of its own story. Happiness pulls it back out and gets it going again.

Sharon, from whom I learned lovingkindness meditation, would end our teacher-student interviews by saying, "Remember, Sylvia, be happy!" For a long time I thought it was the casual "Have a good day" that Californians routinely say. After a while I realized it was an instruction.

Right Concentration: Softening the Blow

•

The Buddha taught that Right Concentration was the ability to let the attention become absorbed in one single thing. Paying attention with a single focus produces particular qualities in the mind. Especially important is a sense of ease, balance, relaxation—a state traditional texts call "malleability of mind."

I taught a class for a while called "Hand Needlework as Concentration Practice." We met for two-hour sessions in a meditation room. For the first hour everyone sat in silence and did needlework. People knitted, crocheted, embroidered, and worked needlepoint. The only sounds were the click, click, clicking of knitting needles, the swish, swishing of thread through canvas or fabric, and, in the winter, rain. The second hour everyone kept up the needlework, and we talked.

We never spoke about the craft we were doing. We talked about our lives, our fears, our struggles, our sadnesses. We talked to each other out of the space of composure, and we listened to each other out of a space of balance. Everyone agreed that the hour of pretalking concentration practice was what allowed us to share so deeply. Concentration practice strengthens *and* softens the mind. That's not a paradox. It's true.

My very first discovery of the effects of concentration came at the end of a two-week silent meditation retreat in Washington state in 1977. Everything about the retreat was strange and difficult. My body ached from sitting still a lot, I struggled with drowsiness, and I was confused about the instructions.

I began to think of the experience as an Outward Bound of the mind and felt that finishing would be a triumph. As the days passed, my body pains disappeared and I was less sleepy, but nothing dramatic happened. On the last day, had anyone asked me, "Are you different?" I would have replied, "No."

That evening, after the silence was ended, I phoned my husband in California to arrange to have him meet my flight. During our conversation, I asked about my father, who had been feeling peaked before I left. "Since I need to be honest with you," he said, "I'm sorry to tell you that your father has cancer, a kind that isn't curable." In that moment, I discovered I *was* different.

Bad news usually feels like a sledgehammer blow to the head. In the moment I heard the news about my father, I knew I was absorbing it in an unusual way. It wasn't that I didn't feel sad. I felt terrible. My father was young, vigorous, and my good friend. The news felt like a sledgehammer, but one where the blow falls on a mattress instead of a brick wall. I trembled, but I didn't crumble. I felt pain and very deep sadness. Then I joined some other retreatants and drank tea.

I have no desire to fix my mind so it will not feel saddened by loss. I want to feel deeply, and whenever I am brokenhearted I emerge more compassionate. I think I allow myself to be brokenhearted more easily, knowing I won't be irrevocably shattered.

Right Mindfulness:
My Father and Raiders of the Lost Ark

•

Mindfulness is the aware, balanced acceptance of present experience. It isn't more complicated than that. It is opening to or receiving the present moment, pleasant or unpleasant, just as it is, without either clinging to it or rejecting it. There are three ways, I think, to understand the purpose of mindfulness practice.

The first way is to see how it leads to wisdom. As a person is increasingly able to stay alert and balanced from moment to moment, the fundamental truths of life experience will present themselves as insights. As insight grows, the teachings promise, the habitual tendency of the mind to continue to cling to what is essentially ungraspable diminishes, and suffering lessens.

The second way to understand how practice works is that the very practice itself deconditions the mind from its habitual pattern of running from discomfort. One sits (or stands or walks or eats or whatever), hour after hour, *practicing* remaining calm and alert through the whole range of body and mind states that present themselves—all the while *not doing anything* to change experience but rather discovering that experience is *bearable*. Thus one comes to see that the practice itself is an antidote to the usual flurried reaction of the mind to each new moment.

The third way is to think of mindfulness practice itself *as* freedom, rather than *leading to* freedom. Any moment of clarity undisturbed by the tension of judging or preferring, rejecting or desiring, is a moment of freedom. We have only moments. Now is the only time we ever have. Cataloging and stockpiling moments of freedom now for comfort in the future might be good reminders, but they don't guarantee freedom forever. Anticipating future freedom may condition Right Aspiration or Right Effort, but if it creates striving in the mind now or a sense of neediness or incompleteness in the mind now, there is no freedom now.

Probably many meditators, Buddhist and otherwise, know the story of the monk being chased by a tiger toward the edge of a cliff. He leaps off the cliff, grasping a vine that has grown over the edge. Below him is a long drop to certain death, above him is the snarling tiger. As the monk swings in midair, a mouse begins gnawing at the vine above him. His position is one of utter precariousness. Growing out of the cliff in front of him is a wild strawberry, which he picks and eats. He says, "This strawberry is delicious."

My father died of multiple myeloma, a cancer that can be treated but not cured. During the seven years of his illness, he managed his diminishing vigor and increasing pain with steadfast stoicism. He accommodated his disability with cane, then walker, then wheelchair—all the while keeping up his vigorous social life. We talked openly and often about the inevitability of his death in the near future, and he seemed reconciled to it without being hopeless or desperate. We joked about which of his grandchildren's households seemed to him the most congenial in terms of a choice of rebirth for him, if it turned out that he really got to choose.

One day, when his illness was quite advanced, his spirits seemed particularly flagging. The day loomed long before us, and I said, "Let's go to a movie." He looked at me, seemingly incredulous, and said, "You know, I'm *dying!*" I said, "Yes, I know, but not today." We saw *Raiders of the Lost Ark*. We both loved it. We had dinner at the Pacific Cafe, his favorite restaurant. The next day he developed pneumonia and needed to be hospitalized. A few weeks later he died.

3

Hindrances to Clear Seeing

Larry King and the Swami

•

It's probably a sign of the times, but I've gotten some of my spiritual information from television talk shows. I remember watching Larry King interviewing a swami in the Hindu tradition. I don't remember exactly what the swami said, but I remember his demeanor was calm and unruffled. Although the phone calls from viewers were often either antagonistic or, at the very least, skeptical, the swami kept a clear and contented presence about himself, responding to each question with clarity, precision, and even quiet humor. Larry King is an interviewer known for the directness of his style and his probing questions. At one point he leaned across his desk and looked into the swami's unblinking eyes. He said to him, "How did you get it so quiet in there?" The swami replied, "It *is* quiet in there. We just all ruffle it up so much."

Here is a test that you can now do in the privacy of your own home to prove the correctness of the swami's insight. Choose a time when you are quite alone and in good health or at least free from bodily pain. Make sure you're neither hungry nor sleepy. Pick a chair you are comfortable sitting in. Sit down in it. Enjoy feeling comfortable. You can keep your eyes closed if you want, or you can open them, look around, and enjoy looking around. Enjoy feeling comfortable. Don't do anything else but enjoy feeling comfortable. Spend at least fifteen minutes enjoying feeling comfortable before you turn the next page. Then, turn the page.

- So, did you feel comfortable the whole fifteen minutes?
- Did you just sit and enjoy feeling at ease and comfortable?
- How long did it take before thoughts arose that disturbed your comfort?
- What kind of thoughts were they?
- Did you have desire thoughts?
- Did you think to yourself, "I wish I'd chosen a more comfortable chair to sit in; this is not the best chair I have. The next time I do this experiment, I'll sit on a really comfortable chair"?
- Did you have irritable thoughts? Did you think to yourself, "Phooey, my neighbor is mowing the lawn. I could have been sitting here perfectly happily enjoying my quiet fifteen minutes if that irritating sound wasn't happening."
- Did you think fidgety thoughts? "Hmm, sitting still isn't as comfortable as I thought it might be. Perhaps I should try taking a walk around the block. I forgot to return Suzie's phone call; I should have phoned before I sat down, and now I'm worrying about what she's thinking of me. What if she doesn't want to be my friend anymore because I never call her back on time?"
- Did you start to fall asleep? Did you think to yourself, "This is so boring. This might be all right for swamis in India, but if this is what meditators do, I'm not sure I'm cut out to be a meditator. Maybe I'll just take a little nap now for the rest of the fifteen minutes."
- Did you think, "This is a stupid exercise. What could this possibly have to do with getting enlightened? I knew I made a mistake buying this book. I'm always doing things like that—making ridiculous, impulsive decisions."

Did you have thoughts like any of the above? Some of them? *All* of them?

Fundamentally, the swami is right: it *is* quiet in there, until it gets stirred up. But there is no willfulness or purposefulness about stirring it up. We don't mean to complicate life for ourselves. It's not naughtiness of mind; other people's minds don't stay quiet any better than ours do. It's in the nature of mind to be stirred by confusing energies, like winds that blow back and forth across the surface of a clear pool, disturbing the visibility. Becoming a meditator doesn't mean stopping the ripples of the waves. Probably totally realized masters can see through all the ripples all the time. Regular seekers like myself are really happy if they can remember that they're just ripples and that there is another side.

Albuquerque Mind

•

We tell stories to ourselves over and over and over again. We bewilder and frighten ourselves, forgetting that the dismay and the fear are always about what *might have been* or what *might yet be* but what isn't happening *now*. We also forget that what's happening now is not going to be happening for very long.

I was teaching a meditation course in Albuquerque a few years ago, in a room with a huge window across one wall. From where I sat, I could see a vast mesa leading to the beautiful Sangre de Cristo Mountains in the distance. It occurred to me that the weather outside, blowing across the mesa, seemed to change dramatically from the beginning to the end of each meditation period. When I closed my eyes, the sun might be shining, and when I opened them again forty-five minutes later, a blizzard might be swirling around the building. When I closed my eyes in the blizzard, I might open them to find it was raining. And then, very soon it seemed, the sun would be shining but accompanied by strong winds whistling around the building. Suddenly the wind would stop, a rosy twilight would magically cover the mountains and the mesa, and a light, quiet snow would fall.

I thought to myself, "The weather is just like the mind." I looked at the group of twenty-five meditators sitting around me, their bodies still and their faces serene. And, because I knew each of them a little bit and I know myself well, I knew I was seeing only half of the picture.

I imagined the following cartoon. I pictured five seated meditating figures, bundled up in blankets and shawls, eyes closed, faces serene, distinguishable from each other only by their size and shape. Everybody's face would be just the same. And over each of these figures would be a big cartoon bubble with a picture in it and little bubbles leading down toward the figure below it, so you would know the contents of that bubble are filling that mind. I imagined one bubble filled with ice cream sundaes and pizzas. Or a Hawaiian beach with swaying palms. Or powerful sex (though I didn't know how I would draw that!). Another bubble would have a war or people fighting or be filled with the typewriter expletives #&*@#$% that let you know people are saying unprintable words. Another bubble would be murky and cloudy. Another bubble might have thunder and lightning or perhaps a volcano erupting in the middle of it. Another bubble might have a bewildered person shrugging the shoulders, palms uplifted and open to show, "I don't *know*." Maybe the "I don't know" bubble would have the background filled with question marks. Then I imagined I'd put a sixth figure in the picture, sitting under a bubble with nothing at all in it.

The point I wanted to make with that picture is *not* that the person with nothing at all in her or his bubble is lucky. In fact, my fantasy was that I'd write a whole book where each page would have the same picture. All the same people would be huddled in their blankets, and their faces would never change. Only the contents of each person's bubble would change. It would be the mind equivalent of musical chairs. Instead of same people, different chairs, it would be same people, different mind states, because that really *is* what happens. Mind states come and go. Even quiet mind states.

Every single human being experiences all the different mind energies, the predictable storms of the human mind. These mind states reflect natural energy ebbs and flows and the mind's normal responses to pleasant and unpleasant experiences. They are totally natural. They do not need to be frightening or even particularly troublesome. If we were moving to another planet, it would be helpful if someone would clue us in about the kinds of storms they have there so we could prepare ourselves. People on this planet also have an easier time when they know how to work with all weather contingencies.

The Limited Menu of Disturbing Mind States

•

In traditional Buddhist texts the five energies of Lust, Aversion, Torpor, Restlessness, and Doubt are called "Mind Hindrances." They are called hindrances of the mind because they obscure clear seeing, just as sandstorms in the desert or fog on a highway can cause travelers to get lost. They hinder the possibility of us reconnecting with the peaceful self that is our essential nature. They confuse us. We think they are real. We forget that our actual nature is not the passing storm. The passing storm is the passing storm. Our essence remains our essence all the time.

Five different energies seem like a limited menu, but they present themselves in an infinite variety of disguises. Ice cream sundaes are different from pizzas are different from sex, but fundamentally they are all objects of the lustful desire. The same energy of aversion fuels our annoyance with our neighbor for playing a radio too loud and our annoyance with our president for not running the country better. Grumbly mind is grumbly mind; sleepy mind is sleepy mind; restless mind is restless mind; doubtful mind is doubtful mind.

The fact that it's in the nature of minds for storms to arise and pass away is not a problem. Living in a place where the weather changes frequently is not a problem. It does, however, require having clothing to suit different climate challenges and the wisdom to stay indoors when the weather gets bad. It also helps in keeping the spirits up to remember that the weather is going to change. Our difficult mind states become a problem only if we believe they are going to go on forever. Then, because they are uncomfortable energies, they start to frighten us.

We have two kinds of fears. One is a fear that whatever is going on is going to go on forever. It's just not true—nothing goes on forever. The other is the fear that, even if it doesn't go on forever, the pain of whatever is happening will be so terrible we won't be able to stand it. There is a gut level of truth about this fear. It would be ridiculous to pretend that in our lives, in these physical bodies, which can hurt very much, and in relationships that can hurt very much, there aren't some very, very painful times. Even so, I think we underestimate ourselves. Terrible as some times may be, I believe we can stand them.

Because we become frightened as soon as a difficult mind state blows into the mind, we start to fight with it. We try to change it, or we try to get rid of it. The frenzy of the struggle makes the mind state even more unpleasant.

The familiar image is a children's cartoon character, like Daffy Duck, walking along freely and suddenly stepping into taffy. In a hasty, awkward attempt to extricate himself, he might fall forward and backward and eventually be totally stuck in the taffy. Even children see a better solution.

The best solution would be the nonalarmed recognition, "This is taffy. I didn't see it as I stepped into it, but I felt it after I got stuck. It's *just* taffy. The whole world is not made out of taffy. What would be a wise thing for me to do now?"

Soup with a Fork

•

We create big problems for ourselves by not recognizing mind energies when they arrive dressed up in stories. They are like the neighbor's children disguised as Halloween ghosts. When we open the door and find the child next door dressed in a sheet, even though it looks like a ghost, we remember it is simply the child next door. And when I remember the dramas of my life are the energies of the mind dressed in the sheet of a story, I manage them more gracefully.

Here's an exercise to show that it's the mind state, not the event itself, that determines our experience:

First Scenario

You've been in a relationship, and the relationship has gone sour. You and your partner are both disappointed that the relationship hasn't worked out and dismayed and angry with the other person for not having lived up to your expectations. You meet for one last day to try to talk things over. You go to the beach to get away from it all, and, as the day goes on, each of you remembers more and more painful ways in which the relationship has failed. You feel exhausted and angry. On the drive back to the city, because both of you are hungry, you stop at a restaurant for dinner. Your partner eats the soup with a fork. You think to yourself, "This is even worse than I thought! This idiot eats his soup with a fork!"

Second Scenario

You fall totally in love. The other person loves you with equal passion. You go to the beach for the day. You lie in the sun, you read Rilke, you splash in the waves, you make love. On the

•

drive back to the city, you are both hungry so you stop in a restaurant. Your partner eats the soup with a fork. You think to yourself, "What a cute idea! Eating the soup with a fork!"

I think this is what people mean when they say, "We create our own reality." I used to have trouble with that idea when I first heard it in the seventies. Hard as I try, I cannot create the reality of the sun rising tomorrow in the west, and I cannot create the reality of the people I know with illnesses being miraculously cured. But one reality I can create–the point of view I bring to any experience.

Lust

•

The energy of lust traditionally tops the list of disturbing mind energies. It's a challenging and interesting energy to start with, because the word itself has come to carry somewhat lascivious overtones. When people mention that they are lusting after something, we don't immediately think they mean ice cream or pizza.

Lust is embarrassing. I once asked the students in a class I was teaching on difficult mind energies if they could name the energy that posed the most difficulty for them in each of their lives. As we went around the room, the largest number of people mentioned anger or aversion as their most troublesome mind state. It did not seem like a hard thing for them to admit, nor did it seem surprising or disturbing to the other students to hear it. Finally, one man said, "Well, I think that lust presents me with the most difficulties." Though I think no one moved, it seemed there was a palpable cringe. Nervous laughter erupted all over the room. Suddenly, this mild-mannered, genial, professionally respected person had become unwholesome around the edges.

Even though traditional texts do talk about lust in terms of sensual energies, I think it makes the most sense for us to think of it as the energy of wanting anything at all. It's the energy of feeling one cannot be happy unless one has some particular thing. It's a sense of neediness in the mind. Did you ever have that feeling? You get up and you look in the refrigerator, and, as you are standing there with the refrigerator door open, you don't know what you want, but you have the sense you want *something*. It's much the same energy that causes us suddenly to turn on the television set and use the remote control to flip through all the channels just in case something interesting is happening.

Needy mind is just needy mind and can exist quite apart from any biological need. Some years ago when my granddaughter Leah was two years old, her baby brother was born. Her other grand-mother and I stayed with Leah on the one night that her mother was in the hospital. We took *terrific* care of her. She knew us both well, and Noemi and I were being totally devoted to her comfort. Nevertheless, in the course of the evening, it became clear that Leah felt her mother's absence. She would say, "I need juice," and we would get her juice. Then she would say, "I need a cookie," and we would get her a cookie. After a while she might say, "Now I need a book," and later, "Now I need a puzzle. I need that doll. I need an apple." At one point Noemi and I looked at each other and realized that Leah was just *needing* something. Noemi said, "Le falta algo" (she's missing something). Leah was feeling the energy of missing something, but she didn't know what. Also, she had no way of saying, "I feel the energy of need and desire, but I don't know what I need."

Sometimes needy mind arises in response to lack, as it did in Leah's case; sometimes it arrives seemingly out of the blue. But it's not out of the blue; it's usually in response to contact with some-thing pleasurable. Have you ever walked by a bakery and become aware of a particular smell wafting out? Just before you smelled that smell, you weren't hungry. All of a sudden, tremendous hunger arises. This is not capriciousness of mind; it's just how the mind op-erates. In contact with pleasant experience, desire arises. Nor is it necessarily naughty to act on desire; sometimes desires are whole-some, especially sense desires. It would be ridiculous to expect that every time we got hungry we would say, "This is just desire aris-ing," and not do anything about it. Ignoring sexual feelings rather than making skillful, conscious choices doesn't work very well ei-ther. Sense desire is one of the periodic energies that fill the mind and captivate the attention. Making wholesome choices about sen-sual desires is part of relational life.

Some desires are more complicated than straightforward bio-logical needs for food or sex. These are desires for pleasant experi-ences. I like to read *Smithsonian* magazine. A new one arrives at my home every month, and in the back of each issue are ads for improbable tours to very faraway places. I might find that quite suddenly I am seriously considering a seventeen-day voyage to the North Pole. Five minutes before I read that ad I had not been thinking of any trips at all. What's more, in all my life up until that point, I hadn't longed to see the North Pole; yet, suddenly, here is an ad so well written that I am seriously looking at the cost of it and wondering if I can negotiate my schedule to meet the trip's timetable.

Catalogs and brochures that come in the mail also can arouse the energy of lust. Every day I get catalogs for items I am not particularly interested in. The covers are so seductive that ordinarily I decide to at least browse through. As soon as I look in them, inevitably I see something so unique that I begin to consider whether I need it. Or I might decide that although I personally don't need it, it's the perfect present for someone I know. Even if it's not that person's birthday, I begin to think about when his birthday is or decide I could put it away for a holiday gift. All of this makes sense, because the way the mind works is that in contact with pleasant experience, we feel a kind of pull, an energy of wanting, and the mind moves toward pleasant sense experiences.

Even when no particularly pleasant experiences are around, the mind is quite capable of recalling images of pleasant experiences and then wanting them. It's incredible to me to find how much the mind can think of desiring in the middle of a monastery. I have spent a lot of time in monasteries doing meditation practice. The food is plain, and the circumstances don't allow for many different activities. In spite of this, I have designed entire wardrobes of more comfortable clothing that I might bring with me to a retreat at some mythical time in the future. I have imagined knitting a warmer shawl; I've envisioned buying a bench or a cushion that will be more comfortable than the one I am using. Even though the range of things available to construct desires out of is narrower, the mind works away at it. I imagine my experience would be much enhanced if there were a different cereal at breakfast or another brand of tea. Depending on how satisfying my meditation practice is, I might find myself thinking immediately after lunch about the menu possibilities for the next meal. I don't think my mind is worse behaved than anyone else's mind; it's just the nature of the mind to scan the horizon for possible pleasant experiences and then dwell on them. It's part of our conditioning.

Sometimes the energy of desire in the mind causes us to fall in love all of a sudden. When the mind and body are full of lustful energy, people look more attractive to us. We begin to construct romantic or erotic fantasies about people, not on the basis of who they are but on the basis of how we feel. This is an especially tricky phenomenon. It happens a lot in meditation retreats when people have taken a vow of silence and therefore have no way of checking out with other people whether they are compatible. People feel stimulated in their minds and bodies, and suddenly, quite dramatically, feel as if they have fallen in love with someone they don't know at all, based on how she walked into the meditation hall or how he eats his food. I myself have fallen in love with the most improbable people just because they have walked into my field of vision while I am feeling particularly and delightfully filled with the energy of lust. I have fantasized scenarios of running off with various people. The whole thing has been ridiculous, since I am a married woman with no intention of carrying on with anyone. Also, the people I fell in love with were usually people I knew something about and who I was aware were also otherwise engaged. The whole scenario was an exercise in futility. Nevertheless, the mind suddenly hones in and decides that this is the relationship of the decade, this is the soul mate I always needed. It's amazing how the mind can make a whole story out of simple body and mind energy.

The energy of lust arises, we look around, and we say, "Boom, this is what I want." It's not really a problem—it's actually funny. It only becomes a problem if we forget to notice it, if we take it seriously.

None of this means that we shouldn't fall in love. Falling in love is wonderful. It probably means that when we fall in love we should wait a bit to make sure that the one we've fallen in love with is not simply an imagined person constructed out of our own desires.

The Buddhist teaching on lust is probably the equivalent of the Eastern European myth that, if you swallow a chicken heart whole, you will fall in love and spend the rest of your life with the very next person you meet. Apparently, this happened to lots of people. Having swallowed the chicken heart and being in that excited, erotic mood, the next person they saw looked very good to them. Being a meditator means cultivating the space in the mind to reflect about what a wholesome and dependable response would be.

The antidote for the hindrance of lust is restraint. *Restraint* sounds almost Victorian these days. I feel a little self-conscious when I use it, because I think I begin to sound like my grandmother, for whom even speaking certain words was an immoral act. But *restraint* is a great word. It means waiting around long enough to see two things.

The first thing one hopes to see is whether or not the object of the desire is wholesome and whether or not acting on the desire would be a moral, responsible, and appropriate thing to do. The second thing that waiting around allows us to see is that the desire itself is just a mind energy. It's a mind energy that colors our feelings and motivates our behavior, but if we recognize it as just an energy, we realize it's not an imperative to action. It's not a demand; it's a suggestion. If the desire is wholesome and the time is appropriate, we can act on it. If the desire is not wholesome and the time is wrong, we can restrain ourselves, and the energy will pass.

The Antidote to Lust: Sylvia's Buddhist Version of Eve's Version of Zalman's Story

•

This is a fable that explains how the difficult mind energy of lust can be overcome by concentration practice. As is the custom in storytelling, this fable has gone through various transitions as it has been retold by each new storyteller. I don't know its origin, but I received it from my friend Eve, who heard it from Rabbi Zalman Schachter-Shalomi, so it now becomes a Buddhist story with Hasidic ancestry.

Once upon a time, before we all were wise, in a land where there were still beautiful princesses whose hearts were asleep and ordinary men of narrow vision, a young man fell in love with a princess from afar. His lust for her filled his mind. He was convinced that they would meet and marry. He imagined the many children that she would bear that he would sire.

One day the princess and her retinue passed in royal parade, and the young man, his limited vision further obscured by his lust, burst through the crowd, fell at her feet, and exclaimed, "When will we be together?" The princess, in complete disdain, replied, "In the cemetery!" by which she meant, "Never in this lifetime, you fool!" The young man took her words seriously, went directly to the cemetery, and waited.

He waited and waited and waited, oblivious to time, with singularity of purpose and steadfastness of heart.

And, as he waited . . .

his mind became so steady and so single focused that it filled with rapture and light, dispelling all aversion and particularity, and he loved everyone, all beings, without reserve. And people felt his love and came to him for blessings.

And, as he waited . . .

he met Death. Indeed, Death was his most frequent visitor, coming as it did at all hours, bringing with it all manner of folk, old and young, rich and poor, attractive and unattractive, loved and unloved. With absolute clarity, the young man awoke to the fleetingness of life, to the inexorable march of time. He awoke to the suffering of beings grasping endlessly at the ghosts of empty experience. And he became wise. And people felt his wisdom and came to him for blessings.

The princess, now married, was childless, and hearing about a sage renowned for blessings, came to ask to be granted a child. And the man, in the boundless happiness of freedom, called forth the intercession of all the wish grantors on all the realms, and she became the mother of many children.

Aversion

•

The opposite of lust is aversion, the energy of anger and negativity. Aversion isn't pleasant. The Buddha spoke about anger as a poison in the mind, like venom that clouds the mind. Unlike the mind filled with lust that looks around for something to satisfy a need, the aversive mind wants to get rid of something.

Sometimes people think anger feels pleasant, because it is a very stimulating kind of energy. A person whose mind has been sleepy or numbed suddenly feels vital and awake. Feeling angry sometimes makes us feel quite powerful, especially when we feel our anger as righteous indignation. Ultimately, though, anger is just a big mind flurry, and it makes us tired and confused.

"What shall I do with my anger?" is one of the questions I hear most often. When people begin to suspect I am about to suggest that the overt expression of anger is unnecessary, they often become nervous and defensive in advance. I think people are frightened that giving up arguing and fighting will make it impossible for them to communicate candidly. I love teaching people that if you *deliver* the message without anger, you can say anything you want to anybody in the world, both making your point and feeling heard. The message could include the fact that you feel or felt angry, but it need not be a current demonstration of that anger.

In the *Vinaya,* the compilation of rules for monks that is part of Buddhist Scripture, the Buddha taught the following guidelines for the expression of anger. He said:

> Before admonishing another, one should reflect thus . . .
> In due season will I speak, not out of season.
> In truth will I speak, not in falsehood.
> For his [her] benefit will I speak, not his [her] loss.

Gently will I speak, not harshly.
In kindness will I speak, not in anger.

For many years I have kept these guidelines on a little card in my office, and I often show it to couples who come to see me about relationship problems.

I love the idea of "in due season." It reminds people that they don't need to express their angry feeling immediately and that choosing a better time might, in fact, allow their partner to be more receptive to their message. "In truth" means, to me, taking enough time to reflect about what we are *really* upset about instead of presenting the more superficial stories, as we usually do.

"You *never* put the cap back on the toothpaste tube" probably isn't true. "Often" is probably more true than "never," and it probably isn't the truth that the toothpaste tube is the source of the anguish. "When you don't put the toothpaste cap back on, I feel you are not concerned about my comfort, and that frightens me" is probably nearer the truth.

"Gently" and "kindly" and "for his or her benefit" mean taking time to examine one's intentions before communicating dismay. It means being sure one's intention is to heal the relationship or instruct with compassion rather than to wound in retaliation for a hurt.

Couples sometimes ask to take the card home with them to copy and post in prominent places. I have wished for some years that I knew a wallpaper manufacturer who would produce this new design, so we could all paper our rooms with the Buddha's teaching on expressing anger.

I was at a conference a few years ago when somebody asked the Dalai Lama, "Do you ever get angry?" He said, "Of course. If something happens and I don't like it, if it is not what I want to have happen, anger arises." It was very clear from the tone of voice in which he said it that, although anger arises, it certainly is no big deal. What was understood was that when anger arises, one does the appropriate thing to address the situation and then the anger is gone. It is impossible for me to imagine the Dalai Lama, whom I see as quite likely the person with the healthiest mind in the world, expressing his feelings of anger in some unskillful way.

Becoming aware of the sudden feeling of anger is like having a thermometer in the mind. When I see the temperature jump, I know something has just happened that was either frightening or saddening. When I am skillful, instead of making any overt, angry response, I can spend a moment looking for the source of my fear or sadness. When I see the source, I am most likely to be able to address it skillfully, unconfused by the aversive energy of anger.

Anger is often a big problem for people who grew up in families where the overt expression of anger was an everyday occurrence. They have too much opportunity to practice anger and not enough sense of the other possibilities. Rage becomes, for them, the habitual response of the mind to unpleasant situations. Sometimes people tell me they feel victims of their "wrathful response button." Or worse, people grow to have a bad opinion of themselves because of their "short fuse." People say to me, "I'm filled with rage." I feel sad when I hear that, because I realize that people have identified with a particular mind energy, perhaps even a particularly prevalent mind energy, as if it is their permanent essence. When people begin to see that anger, like any other mind energy, is just a transient phenomenon and therefore workable, they are very relieved. Their opinion of themselves improves. They are able to think, "This isn't *me*, it's just my Achilles heel reflex! I'll just limp along for a moment, and then I will regain my balance!"

Once we see mind hindrances as energies, we are able to deal with them skillfully. We can recognize them, we can understand them, we can make thoughtful decisions about them, and we can act wisely in relation to them. We stop feeling attacked by them. When I've been overwhelmed by a mind energy, I have felt as if a giant hand has come from nowhere, grasped my mind, and shaken it mercilessly. Now, even when I experience difficult mind states that I cannot control, I know their source is in my own mind and that nothing happens externally. Even when a clearly external event has triggered the response of fear or sadness that has manifested as anger, it is essentially the grid of the mind that has shaped that response.

Sometimes the mind seems saddened or frightened or angry with no discernible external event as a precursor; sometimes anger seems to arise just on its own. Sometimes we start the day, and the mind feels as if it got out of bed on the wrong side. It is the mind in a bad mood, the mind spoiling for a fight. There is *some* cause, of course, since everything is conditioned, but it need not be an external event. Perhaps we had a bad dream. Perhaps we didn't sleep enough. Perhaps there was some hormonal shift in the body. Perhaps it's the phase of the moon. Our body chemistry can account for more or less irritable energies in the mind.

Because a grumpy mood that seems to come out of the blue is so inexplicable, I think we go around looking for something to feel annoyed about, some external circumstance to dislike in order to discharge that energy. Even in meditation retreats where people don't know each other at all, complex vendettas are constructed about total strangers in response to a transitory grumpy mood. Suddenly, a particular person becomes the repository of one's personal, internal irritability, because she walked too noisily or he coughed in the meditation hall. That person then becomes someone you definitely do not like, whose every gesture, from that moment on, provides the possibility for you to tell yourself a long story justifying your negative feelings.

It would be ridiculous to suggest that since negative feelings are transitory they should be ignored. Even if, perhaps *especially* if, they are our response to shifting internal chemistries or the vagaries of moods, we need to be alert to their presence. Otherwise, we might believe the interpretation they cast on the events around us, and that might lead us to behave unwisely. We need to remember that whatever mood is present is serving as a grid for our experience.

On the other hand, if anger arises in the mind in response to an outside event, it's helpful to look for either the saddening or frightening aspect of that event and then take whatever measures we can to address the sadness or the fear. Knowing that negativity or aversion is a transient energy never means to ignore it. It means to see it clearly, always, and work with it wisely.

"But It's My Bench!"

•

Many, many years ago I was doing some weeks of intensive meditation retreat practice. In those days I not only used a cushion to sit on but also kept a bench nearby so I could switch to the bench if I got tired of the cushion. I had a lot of anxiety that my body might hurt me, and I felt I needed to have every possible aid with me. I also sat against the back wall of the meditation hall so I could lean on the wall for support if I needed it.

One afternoon, I was sitting quite relaxed at my spot near the back wall, on my cushion with my bench right next to me. Suddenly, I heard some rustling movement near me. I opened my eyes a tiny bit and saw a hand reach down, take my bench, and walk away with it. Then I saw the person who took it put it down at some distance from me and sit down on it. The person was a new arrival whom I had not yet seen at the retreat.

A volcano of irritability exploded in my mind. It was very "righteous" irritability. He had *my* bench! At that moment it didn't matter at all that I had a cushion and that my body was quite comfortable. Nor did it matter to me that there were extra supplies of cushions and benches that I knew were available from any of the retreat managers. That person was sitting on *my* bench. I spent many agitated hours composing recriminating notes in my mind, addressed to the person who had taken my bench. I never wrote a real note, but my mind relentlessly devised every possible note that I might send. The notes progressed from coldly cordial to mildly sarcastic to outright demanding. Every day the same man sat on my bench, clearly not giving it a second thought. Each time I entered the meditation hall, my anger rose to a new level.

As days passed and my bench showed no sign of returning, a new worry that this person would actually take my bench home with him further escalated my anger. I started to dislike every single thing about that person. I disliked the way he walked, how he sat, and how he ate his food. One day, just after a lunch when I had not liked the way in which he'd washed his dishes, I returned to the meditation hall for the afternoon sitting and found that my bench was back in its original place right beside me. The person who had used it was gone. He had apparently arrived at the retreat late and left early. Suddenly my mind cleared. It was as if it had been filled with a storm for five days, and now the storm had suddenly passed.

It *had* been filled with a storm for five days. I realized I had spent all that time in a storm over the whereabouts of a bench I didn't need. The whole experience felt bizarre. I had used up incredible energy. I was amazed. I thought to myself, "Is this the way I do my whole life?"

Sloth and Torpor

•

I have a friend who travels all over the world teaching classes in Buddhist practice in intensive meditation retreats. Her friends know, because she tells them, that her most difficult hindrance is sloth and torpor. When her telephone rings and someone's voice says, "I am inviting you to teach a meditation course in Paris" (or some other exotic venue), her internal voice will respond, "Oh no! So far away! Such a long trip!" and her out-loud response is usually, "Certainly!" She knows that her initial, internal response has come through the flavoring grid of her mind, which finds all propositions, no matter how alluring they might be to other people, somewhat of a chore. She knows that she loves to teach and is a wonderful teacher and that the wisest thing for her to do is override the reflex response with the more considered, skillful response.

Sloth and torpor sound like bad things. They have a ring of immorality about them. I think that to the Western mind they sound like options we have a choice about. For instance, lying or telling the truth are choices we can make; they aren't inherent qualities of mind. Being lazy and being diligent are choices we make rather than inherent qualities of the mind. Sloth and torpor, when they are used in the context of one of the five difficult mind energies, are meant to describe a mind state of low energy. Because mind energies are always changing and fluctuating, low-energy mind states are part of everyone's experience. Some people, for who knows what reason, find low-energy mind states a frequent experience for them. It does not mean that they are lazy people. It might mean, as it does for my friend, that they need to be alert to the presence of the mind state as a transient filter so it doesn't unconsciously affect the choices they make.

Sometimes people whose minds are sleepy and torporous look like wonderful meditators. They can sit for hours on their cushions, looking tremendously concentrated. More likely, they are asleep or at least in some semisomnolent state. The ability to sit long, in and of itself, is not a sign of spiritual progress. A famous, oft-quoted Thai meditation teacher, in response to a student's question about how long should one sit in meditation every day, replied, "How long you sit doesn't matter. I have seen chickens sit on their nests for days at a time, and they don't become enlightened."

Sitting isn't meditating. Sitting is sitting. Sitting with mind composed, with attention alert, and the faculty of investigation receptive to the awakening of understanding—*that's* meditation.

Meditators with lots of sloth and torpor mind states don't need to stop meditating. Recognizing that their mind state is just a temporary and transient experience, they can do all kinds of skillful things while they wait for it to pass. They can open their eyes. They can take deep breaths. They can sit up straight. They can do walking meditation instead of sitting meditation, because nobody falls asleep walking. Most important, they can not identify with the mind state as if it's a reflection of them or their character in any way. They are not slothful people but people for whom low energy in the mind is a familiar experience.

If one thinks of the mind as a gyroscope, essentially moving toward the place of balance and equanimity but constantly shifting and changing in response to what's going on around it, it makes sense that there should be periods of more energy and periods of less energy. They are natural energy shifts of the mind on its way to greater and greater balance.

Restlessness

•

If aversion is the mind looking for a fight and torpor is the mind falling asleep, restlessness is the mind scanning the horizon for the next impending catastrophe. Energetically, it is the polar opposite of torpor. Torpor is low-energy mind, and restlessness is high-energy mind.

Sometimes restlessness manifests as fidgety body, but that only becomes a problem in meditation situations where protocol requires sitting quietly to avoid disturbing other people. What is more problematic is fidgety mind, mind unable to remain calm. It is as if the mind, with energy to spare, looks around for potential sources of worry. People with restlessness as their predominant hindrance become habitual fretters, and, although they are often embarrassed to admit it ("Worrying about things you can't change is so *silly*"), restlessness is a particularly difficult mind habit to change.

I know more about restlessness than any other hindrance, because it has been my predominant hindrance. My mind has the capacity and the tendency to take essentially neutral data and spin it into worry.

SCENARIO

I am on a street corner in a foreign country where my husband and I have agreed to meet at five o'clock. It is two minutes before the hour. I have the thought, "What if he doesn't arrive in the next two minutes? That will surely mean he has been mugged or even killed! Or held hostage somewhere. Or had a heart attack! I wonder where the American embassy is. If he doesn't arrive, I'll go to the embassy. . . ." This thought takes three seconds, during which time adrenaline fills my body, my heart beats rapidly, and I start to sweat. The adrenaline burst intensifies the worry, and more worries arise: "Who do I know in this country? How can I phone our children?" At five o'clock he arrives. I am relieved, and I am tired.

In the mind of a habitual fretter, this type of scenario is commonplace. Only the place names and characters change to suit each particular situation. The sense of restless mind prowling around looking for material to write a story about remains constant.

As a result of my practice, I am a recovering worrier. My mind still makes up terrifying stories, but I am much less apt to believe them. Sometimes I can catch the story-making machine in the act of churning up a new story, and sometimes I can even laugh at it. If I could disengage the worry machine entirely from my mind, I would surely do it. I don't like it at all. But I was born with it, for whatever karmic reasons, and I'm stuck with it. I've come to think of it, and myself, with compassionate affection. I treat it as if it were an unpleasant neighbor who lives in the apartment next door to me and plays loud music in the middle of the night. If I am obliged to remain in my apartment, I have two choices. I can relax and say, "These are very unpleasant neighbors. Perhaps some day they will move out. Meanwhile, I will buy earplugs or a Walkman and tapes *I* like." Or I can fume and call the landlord, send letters to the tenants' association, and get more frenzied about it. It's when I recognize what's going on that I get to choose.

The Woman on the Beach in Guaymas

•

One of my important gurus was a woman whose name I don't know, although I have told her story dozens of times. She taught me the dramatic lesson that my view of life as perilous and hazard strewn is one particular perception, not the only perception. When I realized that she and I saw the same situation in totally opposite ways, I understood that ways of seeing are conditioned by the different lenses each of us wears over our perception. It helps me to remember how my set of lenses colors my life experience, and sometimes I think, "It could be, with someone else's lenses, that this situation would look quite different."

I met the woman on the beach in Guaymas twenty years ago. It was summer, and Guaymas, in the Sonora Desert of Mexico, was very hot. I was staying in a large, air-conditioned, modern hotel. Nearby was a caravan park, where people, including this woman, were camping in small trailers. This woman was young, and she had two young sons with her. John, the elder, was four years old, and the baby was just beginning to crawl. She explained that she didn't like to stay where she lived in Los Angeles in the summertime, so she camped in Mexico for several months, and her husband flew down to join them each weekend in his own small plane.

Everything in her story seemed worrisome to me:

- Being a woman alone on the beach in a foreign country.
- Having to watch a small baby crawling around at the edge of the water while minding a snorkeling four-year-old.
- The problems connected with getting clean drinking water or refrigerating milk and other perishables in that hot climate.
- How close the nearest doctor was—had she even thought about that?

- The danger of her husband flying down to Mexico by himself each weekend.

Indeed, every aspect of her situation provided me with material from which I could construct a catastrophe.

She seemed to be having a fine, relaxed time.

One night we had a huge rainstorm with booming thunder and flashes of lightning that filled the sky like fireworks. The rain was torrential, and I worried, as I looked out of my sixth-floor window, about the possibility of flash flooding and what it might do to the caravan park. By dawn the storm had passed, and I hurried to check up on my woman and her children. The caravan park was a mess! The rains had washed everything outside the trailers all over the beach, and people were busy sweeping up, retrieving their household goods. My woman was also sweeping, her children playing happily nearby.

"How was the storm?" I asked.

"It was great," she answered.

"Did you have any problems with the children?" I looked over at them gleefully splashing in the puddles.

"Oh no," she said. "The baby slept right through it, and John would have slept through it, too, except I woke him up so he wouldn't miss it."

I was stunned. I thought to myself, *"There is another way to do life!"*

I completely got it that she and I took the same data and saw it through different filters. I came out with a catastrophic story, and she came out with a thrilling story. I wanted to change filters with her.

It would be terrific if I could say from that moment on my insight into the filtering nature of disturbing mind states allowed me to have clear understanding of all situations. That didn't happen. It would be easy if we could just change the filters. The mind I acquired for this lifetime is equipped with its own particular set of idiosyncratic filters through which it processes experience.

Even though filters seem permanent apparatus of the mind, seeing them for what they are reduces their power. That is another way of saying the Third Noble Truth of the Buddha, that "The end of suffering is possible."

We can, with practice, begin to decondition the mind from its unconscious reactivity. Even without changing the habitual tendencies, we can be alert to them and work around them. If the mind is clear and steady, we can recognize filters as being *just* filters and choose the most wholesome response.

The woman on the beach in Guaymas was a great teacher for me. Although I was not able to change my behavior in any way at that time, she taught me that another way of responding was possible. There arose in me a tremendous determination to do whatever I needed to do to be able to respond differently.

These days, when my catastrophic mind tapes begin to play, I can usually laugh at them. I would much rather they didn't play at all. I have a big poster of Meher Baba on the wall of my office saying, "Don't worry, be happy." Some days I am convinced this is the ultimate four-word summary of cosmic wisdom. Until the day arrives that I can actually do that, I am content when I find I am able not to take my frets so seriously.

Less Frightened Is Managing Gracefully

•

One of the things I used to tell people as a way of explaining why I practice was, "I want to be a totally fearless old woman." I really do. At this point in my life, I'm not sure I'm going to make it to totally fearless. I'm very happy with "less frightened."

One of the stories I remember from the Zen tradition that was part of my early meditation experience was that of an absolutely fearless abbot. This abbot was the head of a monastery in Japan during the time when hoards of samurai bands roamed the countryside terrorizing everyone in their path. One day, when a particularly terrible warrior tribe entered the city where this abbot's monastery was, the monks fled for the hills along with all the inhabitants of the city. Only the abbot himself remained in seated meditation in the meditation hall. The chief warrior, enraged that his terrifying reputation had not been frightful enough to cause the abbot to flee, burst into the meditation hall and challenged the abbot with a brandished sword. "Don't you know," he said to the abbot, "that I am the sort of man who could run you through with this sword in a moment without blinking an eye?" To which the abbot is said to have replied, "And I, sir, am the type of man who could be run through with a sword in a minute without blinking an eye."

I think my teachers told this story because they thought it would be inspiring. I was more demoralized than inspired, because I felt myself to be so far from that ideal and couldn't imagine it ever being true for me.

I believe our most deeply rooted fears, the ones that have been the most prominent in this lifetime, become so ingrained in our neurological wiring that probably they remain part of our experience until the end of our days. Robert Stolorow, a primary spokesman for the Self Psychology movement, has written that no matter how realized or analyzed the etiology of a fear system is in psychotherapy, whenever the same constellation of events arises, the same frightened response will occur. No matter how lofty our insight, we are fundamentally animals, conditioned by our experiences.

One of the terrifying things of my childhood was my fear that my mother would die. She had rheumatic heart disease and couldn't lie down flat at night. Her lungs would flood with water, and she would need to get out of bed, coughing and struggling to catch her breath. I lay in my bed in the next room listening to her coughing. Coughing in the night was the quintessential terrible sound of my childhood. Coughing in the night remains the Achilles' heel of my neurological system. I "have a thing" about coughing in the night.

Each of my four children, now all grown up, had the standard childhood diseases. They had chicken pox, measles, and mumps. They fell down. They had stitches. They broke arms and legs and needed casts. They had their tonsils out in the days when people were still taking tonsils out. And I was fine with all of it. But if they coughed in the night, I became terrified. It was always hard for me. I had to tell myself, "He just has the flu," or, "She just has a cold." The fact that my hair stood on end and I felt panic stricken was a reflex reaction. I think each of us has our own frightening variation of coughing in the night.

I don't think this is discouraging news; I just think it's another piece of data about how the mind works. Fearfulness doesn't necessarily have to be a big problem if we recognize that our fears are a result of the way we are wired, most immediately from this life and who knows from what other lives. We can acknowledge our fears and work around them. Even if I feel alarmed about something as innocuous as a cough accompanying a flu, I can tell myself, "This is a result of my earlier conditioning." Telling myself that keeps me from taking inappropriate or unnecessary action.

Someone showed me a burglar alarm system recently. It was wired to go off if movement happened in any of the directions its electronic eye was facing. I think there is a way in which people are walking burglar alarms. Our antennae are set to pick up signals from anything that might frighten us. When things are not frightening, we just let them go by as background perceptions. But each of us is triggered, ready to go off, as soon as something we recognize as frightening sets off our alarm. Maybe that's what people mean when they say about themselves in relationship, "We push each other's buttons." Perhaps that's what those buttons are—alarm buttons.

One of the ways we build intimate relationships with other people is by sharing our fears with them, telling them the things that still frighten us. We learn to say to each other, "I'd like you to know this is my alarm button about being left, and I had it installed at a time when my mother wasn't there to protect me from my fear of abandonment." Our partners in relationship, as we begin to describe our own alarm wiring, can begin to acquaint us with diagrams of theirs. "As long as you showed me your alarm wiring scheme, here's a blueprint for mine."

When we begin to appreciate the ways in which people have been frightened in their lives, we can be compassionate toward them rather than angry. Instead of saying, "Oh, I'm so angry I'm stuck with this person the whole rest of my life," we can begin to feel, "Oh, I'm very sad that this person whom I feel so tenderly toward has all these awful buttons. How terrible it must have been for her or him to have needed to install all these alarm buttons for protection."

It's not embarrassing to still have fears. We can be all grown up and still have fears. We share our deepest fears with our closest intimates—often, a spiritual teacher or psychotherapist. If we're lucky, it's our life partner who gets to be our best friend in the fear-sharing department. Fears, spoken aloud, never seem as horrifying as when they are kept secret. I am old enough to have actually heard Franklin Roosevelt say the famous line, "We have nothing to fear but fear itself." I think he was right.

Doubt

•

Doubt, described as "slippery" in the traditional list of mind-troubling energies, turned out to be the most elusive section of this book to write. I am writing about doubt, finally, when absolutely everything else is done. Given the sequence of the book, it should have come much earlier, but each time I tried to write, every good idea I had about it slipped away. I began to have serious doubts that I *could* write it. I told my Wednesday morning class, as I had told innumerable classes before, that I thought I couldn't write about doubt because I didn't have it. Now I think that's exactly wrong. Some kinds of doubt I don't have. Another kind of doubt, The Big Doubt, I certainly *have* had and sometimes *still* have. What an embarrassing thing for someone on the spiritual teaching trail to admit! Unless I admit it, though, I don't finish the book.

We may experience various levels of doubt—everything from personal insecurity to cosmic insecurity. All manifestations of doubt are reflections of the mind "slipping" off the truth of how things are. When we see clearly, we understand that, given the history of all creation, each of us is the only person we could be and the world is the only world it could be. The truth is: "It's all okay." A slippery mind generates false rumors, like "I'm not okay," "You're not okay," and "The world isn't okay, either."

Doubt is subtler than the four other confusing energies. All the others carry with them strong body sensations that give them away. We know what lust feels like in the body, especially particular lusts like appetites for food or sex, which localize in special parts of the body. We recognize strong aversion by the way the body becomes tense or from the feelings of burning or churning it produces. We identify torpor because it shows up as sleepiness. Restlessness appears as a fidgety mind or a jumpy body or both. All the body energies are hard to miss.

Doubt, on the other hand, slips into the mind disguised as demoralizing thoughts. Once past the security gate of mindfulness, doubt acts like an undercover agent, sabotaging faith and trust. It can blithely undermine confidence on all levels, because it does it entirely as an inside job.

I used to say, "I don't struggle with doubt at all, because my parents expected me to be entirely capable." On the level of instilling personal self-confidence, they did a great job. All my life I've thought, "If other people do this, I can do it, too." If I suddenly got word that I needed to learn Sanskrit in six months, I would begin immediately, undaunted.

The very first time I heard Buddhist teachings, long before I had any kind of in-depth understanding of them, I thought, "I'll be teaching this someday." Now that I *am* teaching, I can confess that thought, which at the time was outrageous. That outrageous thought gave me a lot of courage.

I think I passed my lineage of personal confidence on to my children, but I don't recall being aware of it at the time. I noticed how confidence works when Collin, my eldest grandchild, began to show it at two years old.

It was a weekly routine for Collin and me to spend a day together, and on one occasion he and I went to a local shopping mall. The day was unusual because I had sprained my back and was unable to lift anything.

"Listen, Collin," I explained, opening his door and unbuckling the safety belt on his car seat. "I cannot pick you up. I need you to climb down by yourself."

Collin stood up and carefully turned around. He needed to creep back down over the chair to the car floor, make a half-turn, and climb down over the door step to the ground. When he had finished, he looked up at me.

"What a big boy you are!" I said, sincerely.

"I *are!*" he replied earnestly.

I thought his remark was so cute, I told everyone in my family. "I *are!*" became the password for, "I am confident about myself."

Looking back at Collin's tiny parking lot event, I think the significant part was his ability to sustain careful attention, successfully, over a complex set of actions. Traditional Buddhist texts teach that the ability to sustain attention in the truth of the moment is the antidote to doubt.

Personal self-confidence about ordinary tasks in life is the very local end of the doubt continuum. It's true that I'm okay about Sanskrit. It's not true that I'm always okay about life. Cosmic doubt has been difficult for me to acknowledge in myself. I've passed it off as "depth insight about suffering" or "romantic melancholy," variations of "since life is fragile, the cosmos isn't okay."

"I'm okay" is self-esteem. "You're okay," nonjudgmental tolerance, is friendliness and probably comes from mild genes and kind parenting. "The universe is okay," cosmic contentedness, we call faith.

I used to pass over my faithlessness as a badge of honor. "Faith is extra," I would say. Either you know or you don't. "Belief systems are also extra," I would explain, pointing out the Buddha's teachings about the importance of the personal, direct discovery of truth. He *did* teach that taking other people's word for how things are should not take the place of individual practice and personal confirmation, but he didn't say faith didn't count. I made that part up.

Now it seems arrogant of me to have trivialized faith. Who on earth doesn't need faith? Life is so completely complicated and inexplicable and fundamentally out of control. It's fine, of course, just as it is, because it is just what it is. The Buddha taught that the universe is quite lawful. It isn't a mistake. But it's so *mysterious*.

Faith, for me, turns out to be the sustaining quality that maintains mind balance when the slippery energy of doubt obscures the truth. And that slippery energy, just like every other disturbing energy, arises naturally as a mind event. How absurd for me to maintain, "I have no problem with doubt." All my melancholic musings about life are manifestations of doubt. It took me a while to catch on.

Not long ago I had a massive doubt attack. I woke up one morning overwhelmed with the brokenness of life. Why *that* day, and not every day, is speculation. I had received some sad family news the night before, but not awful news. The season was changing to autumn, and dawn came later than usual, but not much later than the day before. The reason seemed irrelevant. My mood was bleak.

I live in the country and was at home with my husband and a good friend of ours, both of them my spiritual friends and confidants and both of them, in different ways, spiritual teachers.

"How are you this morning?" asked the friend.

"I am terrible," I cried. "I am a total fraud–I am going all over the place telling people, 'Peace is possible,' 'Life is embraceable,' 'It's all grief and loss but it doesn't need to be suffering,' and it isn't true; it's *all* broken, and we aren't equipped as humans to bear it, and what if all religion is a fake, and we are telling each other and everyone else big lies?"

Maybe I didn't put it all in one sentence, but that was certainly the gist of what I said over the time it took me to prepare breakfast. Both men listened to me. I wept, and I scrambled eggs. No one tried to disabuse me of my view. No one tried to remind me of spiritual truths. No one tried to comfort me, either. But I knew they were listening.

I kept up my litany of cosmic doubt and self-doubt throughout breakfast. "Look how broken the world is!" I insisted. "Everything's dying. No one has any understanding. Everyone's killing each other. The planet is going down the tubes. It's ridiculous to be preaching happiness. It's not only ridiculous, it's a *lie,* because I don't feel happy. Maybe *some* people have come to the end of suffering, but not me!"

To my husband, my outburst of melancholy was not news. To our friend, it was, and I briefly thought to myself, "This is not good manners, Sylvia." I had no choice, though, and I wept, and we ate, and they listened and said things like, "Have you got any more of those scrambled eggs?" and "Pass the salsa, please."

After breakfast, we washed the dishes. An hour later, someone said, "Anyone want to do some text study?" I said, "Sure, why not?"

It was as if nothing had happened. Nothing *had* happened. Doubt had rolled in and rolled out, like a thunderstorm. No one had flinched. I had sustained it in my attention, they had sustained me with their support, and the truth slid back into focus. It *is* all broken, but it's manageable.

A Multiple Hindrance Attack:
Grape Bubble Gum

•

Usually people who are confused and unhappy feel as if their minds are filled with one particular difficult energy. "I'm filled with anger!" or "I'm burning with desire!" or "I'm besieged by doubt!" When they hear about someone who claims to have had a Multiple Hindrance Attack, they think, "Oh dear, that sounds *really* bad!" Maybe they have the idea the Multiple Hindrance Attack has the same relationship to Single Hindrance Attack as pneumonia has to sniffles. Actually, every hindrance attack is a multiple hindrance attack. Think about it.

Suppose you fall in love with someone. Lust fills the mind. You think about that person all the time. For a while, it's quite pleasurable. Then, as your work piles up in front of you and your boss is getting annoyed, you think, "I'd better shape up." Aversion arises. "I'll put these thoughts out of my mind." But they stay. Attempts to put the thought, the love-object, out of the mind are ineffective. "I wish these thoughts would go away." By now, the work is even more piled up and agitation is arising because the loved person has not telephoned as she or he promised. Doubt arises. "Once again, I have made the same mistake of falling in love with someone who doesn't care about me. What an idiot I am!" More agitation. "Here comes my boss! The work isn't done! My mind is in a turmoil!" Torpor takes over: "I am exhausted!" There–five difficult mind states, all cascading in, one after the other, once the first one has gotten a foothold in the mind.

Maybe it seems a bit dramatic, but it's true. Check it out in your own experience. It doesn't matter which difficult mind state makes the first entry onto the mind scene. Behind it trail the other four, in varying order, depending on the set of circumstances.

Here's another example: Pretend you go to the opera with a new friend whom you hope will like you. It has been a long day, and torpor fills the mind. The music is not rousing, and you start to feel your eyelids closing. "What a bad impression I am making," you think. "And this friend paid so much for the tickets!" You get angry at the torpor. "Get out of my mind; I'm making a terrible impression!" The torpor continues. Agitation arises in the mind. "I'll never make it to the intermission. I'll slump over right here and probably snore, too!" You passionately wish for the end of the evening, and then the mind wonders whether the evening might have an erotic end. Suddenly, the mind wakes up with the erotic thought. "Oh, good," you think. "Finally I am waking up! Now if I can just keep my mind on these sexy thoughts, I'll be able to stay awake. . . ." The scene ends. Your friend says, "What did you think of the opera?" Alarm arises—you weren't even there!

I had a Multiple Hindrance Attack on October 31, 1985, in Barre, Massachusetts, over a piece of grape bubble gum. It was Halloween. I had been practicing meditation intensively for some weeks in a wonderful monastery that says "Lovingkindness" over the front door. I was in a wonderful mood. I felt serenely ecstatic, if that exists as a possibility. I was full of delight about my practice, and I had terrific confidence in myself. I was seeing things with incredible clarity and figured I was well on my way to keeping it that way.

When I entered the meditation hall for the last evening sitting, I was surprised and delighted with how beautiful it looked. The resident staff of the monastery, the people who looked after the retreatants' needs, had decorated the room for Halloween. All around were jack-o'-lanterns, carved with great artistic care and aglow with candlelight.

As I approached my place in the room, I noticed the staff had put a candy on each person's meditation cushion as a Halloween treat. "How lovely," I thought. Then I noticed that the treat on my cushion was grape bubble gum. I don't like grape bubble gum. I had a moment of aversion. I did not want the grape bubble gum. Other people had better stuff, and I wanted what they had. A moment of aversion, followed by a moment of desire, but never would I have considered exchanging with someone else, so I sat down, grape bubble gum in hand. Then I had another moment of desire. My friend Roger, occupier of the cushion in front of mine, had not yet returned to the room, and I felt like giving him my bubble gum. I imagined he would be happy because then he would have two Halloween treats. "Good thinking," I congratulated myself. "Now you have turned your negativity into a happy state."

I put my bubble gum next to the candy on his cushion and watched him come in, see the two treats, pick them up, and sit down. Immediately, the thought arose in me, "What a dumb thing you just did! How could you have put your gum on Roger's cushion? Now he knows that someone has given him their treat, and he probably thinks he has a secret admirer, and that thought will probably stir up his mind from what I am sure was tranquillity. And I, who presumably am a serious and wise meditator, will have been the cause of his agitation!" By this time, I was totally dismayed about how impulsively I had acted and filled with doubt about how much wisdom I had anyway. Furthermore, I was exhausted. The whole event had taken about thirty seconds. From serene ecstasy to demoralized confusion in less than a minute.

Trivial as the bubble gum is, the story is important. First of all, it's a fine example of the delicacy, the impermanence, the emptiness of mind states. Just like weather, they blow in and out. Good mood. Bad mood. Tranquil mood. Frazzled mood. That familiar "Albuquerque Mind."

In the moments of mental confusion over grape bubble gum, I learned the most valuable antidote to any kind of hindrance attack. The most magic mind balancer is clear seeing. On that Halloween

I saw it all as it was happening. And I laughed! "Sylvia," I said, "you have just had a Multiple Hindrance Attack. So much for your dreams of glory about forever dwelling in joyful serenity. Sometimes it's peaceful and serene; sometimes it's not. Take a deep breath. Smile. Enjoy the fact that you just learned something. Take the next breath. Enjoy!"

4

Clear Seeing: Wisdom and Compassion

Natural Mind

•

When people hear Buddhists talk about emptiness, when they hear the mind described as vast spaciousness, they sometimes get the idea that the untroubled mind is like a cosmic black hole. They may feel frightened and say, "I became more and more relaxed in my meditation, and suddenly I was scared I would forget who I was," or "I'm afraid I'll get lost somewhere and won't know how to get back."

By and large, this doesn't happen. We remember who we are, and usually the effect of meditation practice is that we are more here, now, than we were before, and not in some strange and altered place. The mind spacious and undisturbed does not mean the mind empty of thoughts or perceptions or feelings. It just means the mind *undisturbed*.

When I was a child small towns passed ordinances against "disturbing the peace." I used to wonder what would constitute such a disturbance. Shouting in a public place? Singing in the street? Given our current complex city life, the idea that any place is essentially peaceful, or should be, is wonderfully quaint.

The *mind* is essentially peaceful. For me, that discovery, at least initially, held both bad news and good news, like the punch line of many current jokes. The bad news was that the relaxed mind, the mind free of disturbances, was not necessarily psychedelically exotic. I had hoped it would be. The good news was that contentment turns out to be the most exotic mind state of all and is never tedious or tiresome. We could experience it forever. We *could* experience it forever, because it's our natural mind.

No Cedar Trees, No Burning Bushes

•

Annie Dillard was a major influence on my early meditation life. I read her book *Pilgrim at Tinker Creek* many times. One particular passage in *Pilgrim* moved me tremendously. She describes walking home through the forest to her cabin in Tinker Creek, where she was spending a year in solitude studying nature. Clearly, her mind was very steady, her attention was very focused, and she was living in a state of heightened awe about the interrelationship of all living things. Certainly, this was a mind state conducive to extraordinary realizations.

As she walked home that day, she saw a cedar tree aflame. I knew when I read it that she didn't mean the cedar tree was literally burning up. I assumed it meant the tree had a kind of luminescent or shimmering quality that was extraordinary not in and of itself, but because she was seeing it with extraordinary eyes. She describes the moment as a transforming one and writes that she lives for such visions.

So I wanted my own private version of a cedar tree, my own personal version of a burning bush. I had an idea that, if the mind were steady enough, it would burst out into a kind of Fourth of July fireworks celebration internally, regardless of what was outside. I think this idea was also shaped very much by the opening scenes of the Beatles movie, *Yellow Submarine,* where suddenly everything bursts into color. I wanted everything to burst into color.

As I continued my own meditation practice, from time to time lovely mind and body events did happen to me. I might feel mild raptures in all of my body; my body might shake with thrills of pleasure; colors around me looked a little bit brighter; sometimes leaves looked a little bit sharper. The food I ate on meditation retreats presented itself to me in much clearer tastes than normally.

This didn't mean that a dry apple became a juicy one. A dry apple was still a dry apple, and I knew it. And a lovely taste was a lovely taste, and I knew it. But still, nothing was ablaze, nothing was luminescent, and there were no fireworks of mind. One day, after many years of practice, in the middle of a meditation retreat, I walked outside the retreat center and sat down on a bench near the back door to wait the few minutes that remained until lunchtime. It was a foggy, gray day. The meditation center was an old building in prosaic surroundings, and it was February in California–gloomy and unremarkable. The bench was cold. In front of me stood a tree, still bare because its buds hadn't started to open yet. I thought to myself, "I wonder if this tree could be my cedar tree."

I closed my eyes and paid attention to my breathing. I felt my body sitting on the cold bench; I felt the moist air around me; I felt very relaxed. I began to enjoy the cold bench; I enjoyed its hardness; I enjoyed the sense of cool fog around me; I realized I felt happy. I was even a little hungry, but I realized I was still happy. By and by, the bell rang for lunch. I heard it, and I enjoyed the sound, but no impulse arose in me to get up from the bench and join the lunch line. I kept sitting. Suddenly, I realized this was an odd experience and the fact that no impulse arose in me to do something else was extraordinary. Here was a bell calling me to a potentially pleasant activity indoors in a more pleasant setting, and yet no desire had arisen in the mind to change my situation. I was content. I thought to myself, "Far out! Contentment is the most exotic mind state of all. It's so unusual." Then I thought to myself, "Probably, this is my enlightened moment. Probably, if I open my eyes, that tree in front of me will be shining and shimmering and radiant." Slyly and shyly I opened my eyes. The tree was exactly the same, plain as ever. I was really happy.

From time to time, the desire for a luminescent cedar tree arises again. Usually it happens when I am feeling particularly calm and energized, and I think to myself, "This is so extraordinary, now will be my burning bush." It hasn't happened yet. Actually, I think I'm glad about that. If I saw one, it wouldn't last very long, and then it would be gone, and then I'd have to start looking for the next one, and that would be a problem.

Burning bushes are few and far between. Contented moments are the potential of every moment. Actually, all moments are contented. When they're not, it's because the mind has made a mess of them.

The Three Marks of Experience

•

The Buddha taught three truths about life experience, about *all* life experience, which guarantee happiness and contentment if they are fully understood. All three are obvious, so that when I teach them to people they often say, "That's ALL? *Everybody* knows that!" That's right—they *are* commonplace truths, and it is true that everyone sort of knows them. I believe the point of spiritual practice is that we get to know in a *visceral* way, in a way that causes us to feel less frightened and behave more kindly.

The three marks, or characteristics, of all experience are *anicca, dukkha,* and *anatta. Anicca* means impermanence. Nothing lasts, things loom up on a mythical horizon called "future," pass by as experiences, and disappear into a void called "past." Last year's Super Bowl is in the same void as the Civil War. *Dukkha* means unsatisfactoriness. Since nothing is permanent, there is no place to rest, and life is an ongoing series of adjustments in search of comfort. *Anatta* means no-separate-self. It means the endless stream of experiences arising, unfolding, and disappearing is *all* there is. The idea of anyone separate watching the stream is an optical illusion.

If the truths are so simple and everybody knows them, why do we need any spiritual practice? After all, some people seem naturally wise. For the rest of us, intellectual knowing doesn't seem to be enough. Spiritual practice offers the possibility of knowing in a visceral way, in a way that is transformative. In the Buddhist texts, this transformation is called the development of wisdom. You can't see wisdom, but you can see its reflection. Its reflection is happiness, fearlessness, and kindness.

The Van Driver

•

I was alone with the van driver on a Massachusetts Monday morning, en route to Logan Airport, and, since he looked my age, I guessed he would have children and grandchildren. In very few minutes, we had finished all the statistics—how many, which sexes, how old—and were on to how miraculous genetics is and how grandfather Jim's red hair and Aunt Louise's extreme shyness had turned up in four-year-old Kevin.

From the wonder of it all, the conversation seemed to move naturally on to pleasures: his grandson, the actor; my grandson who speaks Swedish; his family, which loves and cares for each other; mine, which does the same. Very soon we were up to pains: which children had health problems, job problems, relationship problems.

I remarked that everyone's life seems much the same, with assorted joys and woes, only with the names changed. He agreed and smiled as he remembered a time years ago. "We had so much fun," he said, "dressing the kids up for church. The oldest was nineteen when the baby was born, and our family looked wonderful as we walked in, all eight of us.

"Christmas Eve," he continued, "now *that* was really a scene. It all seemed so important at the time, and now it's just as if it never happened. I worked thirty-four years for the post office, too, before I retired and started driving, and now it's as if the whole post office didn't happen, either!"

The Diamond Sutra seems so eloquent when it says we should think of "this fleeting life" as "a bubble rising in a stream, a falling star, a phantom, and a dream." My students, though, sometimes have trouble with concepts like voidness or insubstantiality. It all *seems* real, important, and substantial in the moment. Maybe it's the very eloquence of the poetry in the sutra or its inanimate imagery that is confusing. If we reflect on our own life experience, we know it is true.

Anicca: *Impermanence*

•

Anicca is the truth of impermanence, of the constantly changing nature of all experience. Of course we all know that things change, that nothing endures. No one I know likes to go to the dentist, but everyone goes, more or less relaxed, even for complicated procedures. No one would go at all if appointments were open-ended, with no expectations of when, or even if, we would emerge. We remember things change when we go to the dentist, but we forget when we are confused. Grief confuses us, and loss and sadness frighten us. If we can keep at least a bit of the mind clear about temporality, we can manage complicated, even difficult, times with grace.

This, Too, Shall Pass

•

My fourth child was born when my first child was five years old. I was very happy about my situation, *and* it was overwhelming. I painted the line "This, Too, Shall Pass" across the rafter of my kitchen. It did. Now I recall those days with great affection. When I realize how quickly they passed and how fast everything else in my life passed, I have the sense that I will wake up tomorrow and find that I am eighty years old. When my mother-in-law was old, she used to sigh and say, "One turn around and it's all over!" I used to think that was just her experience of her life. Now I think she was right.

Nothing Stays Comfortable Long

•

The house I live in is one hundred years old. When we moved in there was a handrail alongside the three flights of stairs from the driveway to the front door. The previous owners, elderly folk, were moving to a less challenging house, and since the handrail was unattractive and we were young and vigorous, we took it down.

Recently, we put the handrail back up. We don't need it yet, but many of our friends do. The amazing thing is that it seems like yesterday that we took it down. If I spin a sentimental story about the truth of impermanence, starting with, "My life is passing me by," I might become melancholy. Sentiment in the service of cherishing the present moment might be helpful. Sentiment alone, dwelling on what *might have been*, drags you down.

Phyllis is one of the people I know who needs the handrail these days. When I first met her, ten years ago, she could manage the three flights up to my house easily. Now her body is frail and she needs a special chair in order to sit without discomfort. Last week, I adjusted the pillow behind her back and asked, "Does that feel better?"

"Yes," she replied wistfully, "but nothing stays comfortable long."

Dukkha: *Unsatisfactoriness*

•

It seems a bit like bad manners to say, "Life is unsatisfactory," as if we are complaining about something. In the third grade I got an "Unsatisfactory" in "Works and plays well with others," and I remember it still with chagrin. I suppose I got that poor grade because other people worked and played better with each other. But how can life be "unsatisfactory"? Compared to *what?*

The second characteristic of experience the Buddha taught, that of the ultimate unsatisfactoriness, is an elaboration of the awareness of impermanence. It should be liberating. When we "get it" about temporality, we should also "get it" that holding onto anything, in addition to being painful, is totally futile.

Not one single thing can be counted on to stay put. Once I was teaching a week-long course especially for beginning meditators. Many meditation practices, including the mindfulness practice that I teach, begin by asking people to rest the attention in the experience of breathing. This is because everyone is breathing, and breath is quite plain and easily accessible. Resting the attention in the experience of breathing is usually calming and builds the ability to focus clearly.

I phrase meditation instructions in ways I hope will draw people's attention to the experience of constant change. I do this purposefully, since my hope in teaching people is not that they will just calm down but that they will also develop wisdom, that they will experience for themselves the great liberating truths the Buddha taught. I say things like, "As you let the attention rest in the experience of the breath, be sure to particularly notice how it arises and passes away. Everything that arises passes away."

Days of the course went by, and I continued to give instructions in a way that I hoped inclined people's awareness to the experience of temporality. "As you walk, notice how each footfall arises and passes away." "As you eat your lunch, notice how the appetite you feel at the beginning of the meal disappears as you continue to eat."

Finally, one afternoon, as if in desperation, one of the students interrupted the instructions: "Why do you keep on saying that?" he blurted out. "I can't stand that you say that."

"I say it," I replied, "because it's true."

I do understand his dismay. I shared it myself, for some extended period of time. There was a period in my own meditation practice when the passing away of phenomena was the *only* thing I was aware of. All of life seemed like a painful, irrelevant exercise on the way to death. I had an interview with my meditation teacher one day, and I described how incredibly empty and senseless everything seemed.

"Be very careful, Sylvia," he said, "not to let this insight about unsatisfactoriness condition aversion to life experience."

"Thank you very much," I replied politely, in the style that one uses with respected teachers, assuming they know what they are talking about, and I left the interview. As I closed the door behind me, I thought, "HOW?!"

Not long afterward, still stuck in my senseless-because-it-is-unsatisfactory view, I went with my husband to Hawaii on holiday. What a strange time! Hawaii is meant to be beautiful and romantic. We would sit at an outdoor restaurant on the beach, watching the sun go down. All around us couples were holding hands, smiling at the sunset, no doubt saying romantic things to each other, while I wept copiously! "Another day is over! Everything passes away! It's all empty and senseless!" I guess I wasn't a very fun partner for that holiday.

There is another way to understand unsatisfactoriness without everything becoming senseless. Becoming aware of fragility, of temporality, of the fact that we will surely all be lost to one another, sooner or later, mandates a clear imperative to be totally kind and loving to each other always. People sometimes say about a critically ill person, "Her days are numbered." *All* of our days are numbered. No one knows what number we are up to. Literally, we haven't a moment to lose.

Even if It's Senseless, Mushrooms Matter

•

My friend Alta's life was a lesson to me, and her death was a lesson to me, too. She enjoyed good health for seventy-nine years, then quite suddenly she became desperately ill, and it was clear she would die very soon. She accepted this awareness with her normal consummate grace. That was half the lesson she taught me.

The other half was about what makes sense. On the last day Alta could talk to me, two days before she died, we talked about meaning.

"I'm thinking about the meaning of it all," she said, "and it doesn't seem very important. What do you think?"

"Maybe it's 'much ado about nothing,'" I said.

"Seems like that," she replied, adding, "You did a good eulogy for your father."

"I'll do yours, too."

"I wouldn't want to put you to any trouble. . . ."

"Give me a break, Alta! What do you want me to say?"

"It doesn't matter. Say anything you want."

"How about if I give your recipe for the great marinated mushrooms you make?"

"That's a good idea. They were very good. People liked them a lot."

"Do you remember the recipe? You could give it to me now."

"Not exactly. Look it up. It's in my recipe box. Remember to say they shouldn't be made more than four hours before you eat them. The mushrooms wilt."

Mushrooms are as meaningful as anything else.

Anatta: *Emptiness*

•

The third of the liberating understandings the Buddha taught is yet another elaboration of the law of change. Since everything is change happening, there is no one who *owns* the changes and no one *to whom* the changes are happening. We are verbs, not nouns, experiences unfolding, stories telling themselves as sequels to other stories previously told. Rocky II. Sylvia III. Son of Flicka. Stories related to particular other stories ("conditioned" by them is what the Buddha would have said), but fundamentally related to *all* stories, totally empty of anything separate or unique or enduring.

Cosmic View/Local View

•

I recall reading somewhere that the astronauts who walked on the moon, or perhaps *all* the astronauts who got far enough away to see the whole earth at one time, shared a certain experience. They felt awe and wonder at the scope of stories happening on earth without the additional judgment of good story/bad story that begins the closer we get to home. I have a bit of the same reaction when I travel on the earth but far from my family. The fact that they exist at all seems much more remarkable than any dismay or delight that I might have about them when they are nearby. Spiritual practice cultivates the ability to hold the far-out view in mind, even when we are close-up and personal.

My favorite photo is earthrise as seen from the moon. It's perfect. A great blue and green ball floating in vast black space, hanging right there in its orbit. From that vantage point, the scene on earth is awesome. Creatures being born, other ones dying; plants blooming on one side, plants withering on the other; snow snowing, winds blowing, volcanoes erupting, earthquakes shivering, people talking, music playing. From the moonview, it's incredible cosmic drama. From our usual view, inside the drama, looking up at the moon, it's a different story. It changes from *the* drama to *my* drama and gets to be a problem. If you're far enough away, it's not your story—it's one of the five and a half billion stories.

Remembering the two views SIMULTANEOUSLY is a great challenge. My friend Zalman proposed a scenario to a class I was in twenty years ago, and I've told it to my classes dozens of times since. It describes the delicate tension involved in holding the two views together. He asked us to imagine what it would be like to be in a movie theater for the opening minutes of Alfred Hitchcock's *Psycho*. Janet Leigh gets stabbed in the shower in the first scene. We are so upset we stand up to leave, and a friend restrains us by saying,

"Wait! It's only a movie!" Zalman asked us to imagine further that we sit back down, begin to follow the story, and then have the same friend tap us on the arm every two minutes, saying, "Remember, it's only a movie!" We'd be annoyed. We'd say, "Leave me alone! I'm trying to enjoy the movie!"

Knowing that life is like a movie, with each of us having been handed our particular role to play, doesn't mean we can be careless or indifferent about it. Really fine actors *feel* the parts they play and are gratified by reviews that say their character was fully alive. I want to feel my life fully, play my role as if it is real, and let it go gracefully when it's finished. To do that, I'll need to keep a cosmic perspective.

When my father was dying, I remained at his bedside for his final days. The last few days of his life he was primarily in a coma from which he would rouse himself from time to time. We knew he was dying, and we were making him as comfortable as we could, waiting for the last breath. Every once in a while he would seem to breathe his last: his body would shake and he'd have the kind of apnea that people do when they are dying. I would hold his hand and say my prepared speech: "Go to the light" and "Now is your chance to get out of this body." I'm pleased that I did that; those are all the right things to say when someone is dying. ("You've done a good job in this lifetime." "Everybody loved you." "It's time to move on." "You don't need this old body anymore.") Each time he would struggle with the breath, I would give him the speech again. Then he would relax and fall asleep, and I would go back to waiting. Very near the end, he began again a siege of apnea, and I leaped to my feet, beginning my talk about "Go to the light." He opened his eyes, and he looked at me and said quite clearly, "You know, it's not that big of a deal."

The Sewing Machine Man: Forgetting Your Story

•

The insight of *anatta,* the awareness that no one owns the story, seems most elusive. When we say, "I feel so sad," it surely feels as if there is someone inside who owns the sadness. I met a person once who saw right through his story and was freed of it.

I needed my sewing machine fixed, and since I had moved to a new town I found the local dealer in the Yellow Pages. As I drove up, I noticed a sign in the shop window: "Business is fine. People are terrific. Life is wonderful!" This is an unusual sign for a sewing machine store. It's an unusual sign for any store.

Inside, I found that the walls and countertops were decorated with similar upbeat slogans, the kind I see in key chain catalogs: "When Life Hands You Lemons, Make Lemonade!" "This Day Is What You Received, What You Make of It Is Up to You." The proprietor of the store acknowledged my presence but stayed totally attentive to his customer. He wasn't rushing, so neither was I.

When it was my turn, he was completely helpful. When we had finished my sewing machine business, I ventured a personal, psychologist's remark: "You seem like a very good-mood person," I said. "Was your mother a cheerful person?"

"No," he responded. "My mother was an alcoholic and very depressed."

"I suppose," I continued, "that your father was a good role model for you."

"No. My father had rage attacks, and he beat us up a lot."

"It's a wonder," I exclaimed, "that you turned out so well!"

"I didn't turn out well at all! I was a mess!" He smiled ruefully. "I did terribly in school. I never really learned to read. I got through high school because I got bigger and bigger, so they moved me along."

He didn't seem to mind telling his story, and I continued to ask questions. His situation defied all conventional wisdom.

"After high school things got worse. I did drugs. I got into trouble. Finally, I didn't know what else to do, so I joined the Marines. The first day, they gave us all uniforms, and they gave us all haircuts. Six of us got haircuts at the same time. They faced us all toward the back wall, and they clipped everyone's hair. Then they turned all six of us around, at the same time, to face the mirror. I was scared for a minute. I couldn't find myself! There was no one there whose story I knew!"

For me, that was the most important line of his narrative. "There was no one there whose story I knew!" He went on to explain how, having seen that it's all a matter of what story you "own," he decided to have a new story. The old one, he figured, wasn't serving him well.

He finished the Marines, learned machines well enough to get trained in sewing machines as a civilian, married, raised a family, and ran a small, thriving business. He laughingly told me he still hadn't read more than one whole book in his life. People seem to flock to his store, though. Partly, I guess, it's because he is good at fixing sewing machines; however, I think it's mostly because they like being around his vibes. I don't suppose everyone who visits his shop asks as many questions as I did. I think they just intuit that he knows something special.

The Divine Abodes

•

In traditional Buddhist texts, Lovingkindness, Compassion, Sympathetic Joy, and Equanimity are called the "divine abodes" of the mind. The essence of mind, unencumbered by confusion, is ultimately spacious. It is inherently equanimous, encompassing all things and holding them in an ease-filled balance.

It is from this place of equanimity that spontaneous movements of the mind arise in response to different events. Lovingkindness arises as the spontaneous response to all beings, and compassion arises as response to pain. Sympathetic joy arises in the shared delight of other people's good fortune when we become aware of it. All three of these movements of heart and mind (of lovingkindness, of compassion, and of sympathetic joy) are the varied reflections of fundamental equanimity.

Equanimity is not empty; equanimity is full of everything.

Lovingkindness

•

Lovingkindness, an awkward and somewhat quaint term in English, is the translation of the Pali word *metta,* which means complete and unrestrained friendliness. The Buddha taught that when the mind is at ease, it is friendly, congenial, well-wishing. The mind at ease likes nearly everybody. Even people who, because of who they are or what they do, are very hard to like, the mind at ease accommodates with compassion.

People do special practices to cultivate unrestrained friendliness. Some of these are meditation practices. Others are daily life practices, like smiling at supermarket clerks, helping people carry packages, holding the door of an elevator while the last person dashes in. It might seem, at first glance, that *metta* practice, friendliness practice, is on behalf of other people. It is equally on behalf of ourselves.

Friendliness is not hard. We don't need to *learn* to be friendly. We need to *remember* to be friendly. Children, unless they have been frightened, are friendly. Puppies are friendly. My friend Bob recently discovered that the penguins in the Galapagos are friendly, because they don't feel threatened.

"How am I feeling threatened?" is the question I ask myself when I'm not feeling friendly toward someone. There is always something. When I first began to do conscious *metta* practice, using my meditation time to send good wishes and hopes to all the people I knew, I was amazed to find what a long grudge list I had been harboring in my heart. Nothing very serious—a minor slight here, a mild criticism there, minute blips on my radar screen, which had led me to carefully and secretly file the individuals away under "People I Don't Like Very Much." Like the Lord High Executioner in the *Mikado,* I had a "little list" of "people who never would be missed."

It wasn't as if I had been actively generating ill will in the direction of my list. Indeed, I was surprised at the memories and dismayed at the effect they produced in me, lo these many years later. It also tarnished my self-image. I enjoyed the idea of myself as a splendidly tolerant person, and when that turned out not to be true, I was disappointed.

It was because I was disappointed and because I didn't want to carry secret grudge lists around with me that I seriously undertook goodwill practice toward the people who had offended me.

Very soon my ill-will list began to change. The offenders were no longer frightening to me. For a while, I remembered who was on the list, but the energy of the list was gone. Now, I find I can hardly recall the names.

Nice is another quaint word, but it goes with *friendly*. I did not start my spiritual practice because I wanted to be a nicer person; I thought I already was a nice person. I wanted to be less frightened. I did become nicer, though, *and* less frightened.

My Father-in-Law and Great
Aunt Sarah

•

Directing lovingkindness, or sending goodwill, toward people we feel very good about is usually easy to do. Directing goodwill to your grudge-list people is hard to do. What makes it possible is recalling at least one positive thing about each person on the list, the remembrance of which opens your heart. The key is forgiveness. To do anything less is painful.

On my nineteenth birthday, a month after I was married, my great-aunt Sarah died in Bellevue Hospital after a long, debilitating illness. My father, her only other relative, was out of the country, and so it fell upon me to arrange the funeral. The folks who phoned me as next-of-kin assured me that it would be no problem since Aunt Sarah was a paid-up member of a burial society, and all I had to do was show up at the funeral home the next morning. I was frightened of death, I had no experience with funerals, and my father-in-law said, "I'll go with you."

The funeral home was gloomy, and I felt weird. I was the only woman there. There were clumps of old men, nonrelatives, who apparently hung around so there would be a *minyan,* a ten-man quorum, for prayers. Two old women emerged from a back room and left the building. The director of the funeral home approached me and said, "Those were the women who dressed the body for burial. Now, one of the women in the family needs to go and inspect the body." I must have blanched. My father-in-law said, "*I'll* inspect the body."

Harry Boorstein lived another fifteen years, and mostly my memory of him is a vague, generalized, sense of goodwill, but when I think of him in that one moment at the funeral home, I feel a big hit of gratitude and heart opening. If I remember, at any time, any inept remark he made to me or any thoughtless act he may have done, I have only to recall the funeral home—"*I'll* inspect the body"—and I love him. I treasure the moment because it is my magic key to always loving him, and when I love, I'm happy.

Loving Everyone in the World Is the Easiest Way

•

Half an hour out of Chicago the pilot said, "No cause for worry, folks, but we've lost one of our hydraulic systems, so we'll go back to Chicago and get it fixed rather than cross the Rockies without it." As he spoke, the plane banked around in a wide circle. "It will be about thirty minutes until we're on the ground, so you can sit back and relax."

"Relax?!" I had been reading my friend Joseph's new book on mindfulness meditation when I heard the announcement. Mindfulness is clear understanding of current experience, and my clear understanding was that I was *alarmed*. I picked up the book again, hoping it would divert my attention. "When difficult emotions arise," Joseph had written, "do not try to divert the attention." "Okay, Joseph," I said, and I closed the book.

I thought about what I should do. It occurred to me that I might die, and, about that, I had no choices. I decided to offer lovingkindness prayers for my next-of-kin, a daily ritual of mine. It has a certain established order. "May Grace be happy.... May Nathan be happy.... May Erik be happy.... May Leah ... May Collin ... Emmy ... Johan ... Peter ... Trish ... Liz ... Michael ... Sarah ... Seymour." Thirteen names. I finished them, and we were still flying along smoothly. So I did them again. I began to feel calmer.

The plane began a gradual descent, and although everything seemed normal, we were given instructions to take off eyeglasses and shoes and remove sharp objects like pens from pockets. I began to think of other people outside my list of thirteen whom I also hoped would be well and happy, so I started a list for them. "May Miriam be happy.... May Aaron ... Eugenia ... Henry ..." My mind filled with the names of people whose stories I knew, and I began naming faster and faster to be sure I mentioned each of them.

Out the window I could see the ground drawing closer and closer. The flight attendants demonstrated the brace-yourself position, and we all leaned forward and braced. I thought, "In one minute, I'll either be dead or I won't be dead. Should I do my list of thirteen again? Did I forget anyone I know that I care about? May all beings be happy! May all beings be happy! May all beings be happy!"

We touched down, the brakes worked, and the plane slowed to a stop. The runway was lined with emergency vehicles, lights flashing, and we didn't need them. I learned two things: Loving everyone is easier than loving particular people. It doesn't require remembering who is on the list and who is off the list or who is on the main list and who is on the secondary list. And there is no possibility that anyone has been forgotten.

I also learned that ardent loving wishes for others erases personal fear. I hadn't diverted my attention; I knew what was happening, and I also knew I had exactly the right formula for that situation. For some time afterward I thought, "I want to teach that formula to people so they can use it in the moments before their death." Later on I realized, "I want to teach that formula for *every* moment." *All* our moments are moments before our death, and wishing well is the most fearless way to spend them. Sometimes I think the only thing worth saying is "I love you."

Compassion

•

Compassion is the natural response of the heart unclouded by the specious view that we are separate from one another. Traditional texts describe it as "the quivering of the heart" in response to realizing someone else's pain. I think we feel it as our own emotional system vibrating in synchrony with someone else's. It requires a quiet state of mind. Quivering is subtle.

I boarded an early morning flight once, in Laramie, Wyoming, after teaching a three-day, mostly silent workshop for thirty people. I had worked hard to stay attentive to everyone's experience, and I felt relaxed and content because I thought I had done a good job.

An elderly man and woman took seats next to mine, and as soon as we were airborne, the flight attendant served breakfast.

"We ordered a kosher breakfast," the old man advised the attendant.

"I'll check," she replied, and returned with apologies. "Apparently they have forgotten to put your meals on board. May I give you a regular breakfast and have you see if you can eat any part of it?" she offered.

"No, I'm sorry," the man said. "We can't do that."

I began to weep and was surprised. The situation wasn't critical, and the flight was a short one. Probably I was particularly touched by the fact that the couple reminded me of my grandparents, and I understood their dilemma. From an outsider's view, their situation was an odd peculiarity. From their perspective, it was a nonnegotiable disappointment. Because my mind was quiet, I could feel their pain.

Every pain is important pain to whomever is feeling it. When I was a child, people sometimes said to children who didn't eat their dinner, "Think of the starving children in Europe." I'm grateful no one said that to me. I was, by nature, a nervous eater, and adding guilt and embarrassment to my already uncomfortable state would have increased my distress. People who made that remark probably forgot that, although being hungry is painful, eating when you aren't hungry is also painful. Pain is pain. Ranking it is extra.

We evaluate pain by passing it through our value systems, which are, after all, only opinions. "This is important pain," or "This is trivial pain." When I feel remote from someone's pain, it's always because I've made a judgment about it. Perhaps I think that person's situation is so terrible it must be unbearable, and I am trying to protect myself by denying it. We did it at the movies, when we were young, covering our eyes in the horrifying scenes, saying, "Let me know when this bad part is over." I still sometimes do it, reflexively, in movies when the scene is too grim.

Sometimes I feel remote from someone's pain because I am alarmed by that person's judgment. "How can you be fretting about *this?*" I think to myself. "What you really should be worried about is this other, much more worrisome thing." It's ridiculous to decide what "should" grieve someone else. Everyone's attachments are unique. I have been embarrassed to admit the degree of pain I have felt over attachments that I know, by other people's standards, are trivial. Even without outside criticism, I judge myself harshly. "What a selfish person you are!" I scold myself. "The world is in terrible shape, and you are agonizing about this nonsense?"

Pain is hard to acknowledge directly because there is so much of it. Perhaps our collective alarm that the Buddha was right about life being suffering causes us, sometimes, to try to minimize pain. "Things *could* be worse," well-meaning people say to friends in distress, hoping perspective will be soothing. "At least you have your health." "At least you have your career." "At least you're not in Blank (any country at war)." Or the ultimate spiritual comparison, "In the sphere of the cosmos, what does this matter?" All these are adult variations of "Children are starving in Europe." They add humiliation to preexisting pain and make it worse.

Of course, it *is* true that in the sphere of the cosmos our current heart pain is minute, inconsequential. In that same sphere-of-the-cosmos perspective, everything is *equally* inconsequential. This does not fit our emotional reality. Some people and some issues feel especially significant to us. Also, we don't live in the sphere of the cosmos. We live here.

Remembering the sphere-of-the-cosmos point of view, *remembering* earthrise from the moon, *remembering* the interconnectedness of all beings—all these remembrances make it possible to look more directly at pain. Perhaps it's the necessary perspective for seeing pain clearly, for being able to stand it. Remembering our own special affinities, our own kinship feelings, our own heartbreaks in our personal stories, which seem so real and important, keeps us *in* this world, not *out* of it, caring deeply and acting kindly.

Generosity as a Natural Act

•

I am blown away by generosity that is completely unselfconscious. It is the most concrete example of the Buddha's idea of "nonseparate self." Of course our bodies are, in the physical sense, separate from other bodies, popping into and out of this world at different times and different locations. But the essence of consciousness that enlivens all those bodies is singular. With that awareness, fear vanishes and sharing is a totally natural act.

A woman much younger than I am was dressing next to me in the locker room at the gym. We were talking about the benefits of regular exercise for staying fit and trim, and she added, "I just had some surgery a few months ago, and my doctors are amazed at how fast I've gotten my strength back."

"What kind of surgery did you have?" I asked.

"I gave my sister a kidney. She's a diabetic, and she needed it."

She said it with the same matter-of-fact tone that might have accompanied, "I had an extra bike I wasn't using. . . ." She was completely casual about it. It was just what needed to be done.

I've been thinking for many years about one particular story about the Buddha. In one of his previous incarnations, he was walking along the edge of a cliff and heard cries coming from below. Upon looking over the edge, he saw starving tiger cubs with a mother tiger too weak to feed them. The Buddha-in-progress leaped immediately to his death to provide nourishment for the cubs.

The story was told as a generosity story. It worried me because I couldn't imagine that kind of spontaneous selflessness.

Now I can. I have five grandchildren. For them, I would not hesitate a minute about a cliff decision. I'm not even especially proud of that because it's not a big deal. *Not* doing it would be impossible. What would be a big deal for me is the next step, which is to remember always that everyone's grandchildren are mine. Anyone's grandchildren are *everyone's* grandchildren.

You don't need to have children or grandchildren to have this realization. This is the truth of nonseparate self, and it reveals itself when the attention is focused. I see it happen when a disaster occurs. A plane crashes in the Potomac, and passers-by leap into the ice-filled river just because people are in it–not people they know, just people in need. There is a fire in the World Trade Center building, and people carry a co-worker in a wheelchair down sixty-seven flights of stairs, at great risk to themselves. No one thinks, "I'll do heroism," or "I'll do generosity." We realize, when the attention is sharp, that we are all part of each other, and we become caregivers. Perhaps *generosity* is the word we use as long as we think there are donors and recipients. When sharing is a natural and spontaneous act, we probably call it *compassion*.

I used to think if I began seeing all beings as my kin, it would be a big burden. The opposite is true. When someone I know is doing something admirable I don't feel *I* need to be doing it. She is doing it on my behalf, or *as* me, relieving me of that particular task. Mary and Chodren are being nuns for me, Alex is teaching for me in remote places, Itzhak Perlman is me playing the violin, and Joe Montana is me, too. So is his mother.

Sympathetic Joy

•

Jerry Rice, the San Francisco wide receiver, was interviewed by Al Michaels during the halftime of the Forty-Niners versus Saints game on Monday Night Football. They talked about the various league records Rice already held. Al asked, "Which other records would you like before you retire?" Jerry smiled and said, "I'd like them all." Then Al asked, "Of all the great moments of your career, which stands out for you as the greatest?"

"It was when we won Super Bowl XXIII," Jerry replied. "It was my first Super Bowl, and in the last two minutes of the game, Joe Montana threw a pass to John Taylor, who was in the end zone. John Taylor caught that pass, but I felt as if it was me."

That's sympathetic (or altruistic) joy—such delight in the pleasure of the moment that the focus of the joy is irrelevant. Everyone's satisfaction is shared equally.

I once heard the Dalai Lama teaching about how sensible it was to put other people's good fortune on a par, at least, with one's own. There are, he explained, so many other people that your chances for delight are immeasurably increased if the joys of others are experienced as your own. On this planet, my chances of feeling pleased would be enhanced to 5.5 billion to 1. Those are good odds!

Since the medium of altruistic joy is pleasure and not pain, it sounds like it would be easy to do. It's more complicated than it seems. I think we often feel almost–altruistic joy. Something wonderful happens to someone else. We feel genuine delight. And then into the mind that isn't totally contented comes the thought, "I'd like a little of that particular good fortune myself."

I watch it happen in my mind when I see a sweepstakes commercial showing a person who has just opened her door and been presented with a check for $10,000,000. I have some moments of genuine pleasure as I see the amazed winner laughing and crying with happiness. Then I think something like, "I wonder what I would do if that happened to me."

"Of course," I remind myself immediately, "I would give most of it away. At least 75 percent of it. Maybe 50 percent. Then I'd give the rest to my children. They could pay off their mortgages." Then I remember, "They are doing fine on their mortgages. I'll put it into trust funds for my grandchildren's college education." Then I think, "Hey, it's at least ten years before Collin starts college, and who knows what he will be like at that time or what colleges will be like. Maybe Seymour and I could take one of those three-month freighter trips around the world. Can't do that, though, he gets seasick!" In a matter of seconds, the mind filled with sympathetic joy has become a mind filled with schemes for personal pleasure—all out of nowhere. Before the person on television appeared with her check, I was feeling quite satisfied. Yet it seems the nature of minds, if they aren't completely clear and at ease, to be intrigued by the idea of a little more satisfaction.

I think we assume that other people, on hearing of our good fortune and congratulating us, would like something similar for themselves. Perhaps when we wish the same for them, we acknowledge our own joy and relieve others of any guilt about envy that they might be feeling. I learned this by overhearing wedding conversations when I was a child. The mother of an unmarried daughter, embracing the bride's mother, would say, "And may you continue to have joy from this." The mother of the bride would respond, "And may this come to pass for your daughter, too." The first mother would then say, "From your mouth to God's ears!"

I have been embarrassed, even felt guilty, to find that in short moments after learning of someone's good news in a category in which I have personal yearning, I begin to feel envy. I reprimand myself by thinking, "What's the matter with you, Sylvia? Your cup runneth over. How can you possibly *think* that?"

It's not a question of whether the cup runs over or not. The world is so full of wonderful things, there is no end of things to put into the cup. It's a question of clear seeing. When we see clearly, we see there is only one cup.

In Super Bowl XXIII, when Joe Montana threw that touchdown pass, John Taylor was in the right place. Jerry Rice's mind was also in the right place.

Equanimity Is Full of Everything

•

People often ask if it is possible to be peaceful *and* passionate. I believe it is. I plan to do it. I think the question arises because people have confused placid with peaceful or tranquil with equanimous. *Peaceful* means "not angry." *Equanimous* means "balanced." Neither of them means "blah"!

In the beginning of my Buddhist practice, I used to worry a lot about becoming an emotionless person. I thought I might turn out like someone who had had a steamroller flatten her heart, nonreactive in all circumstances. I believe I shared a commonly held misperception—the idea that spiritual means "unruffled calm." My view seemed to be confirmed by stories my teacher told about people who practiced meditation so intensely that "their interest in sex fell away, and they lived together like brother and sister." I worried, because, although I wanted to be enlightened, I didn't want *that* to happen to me.

Calmness and tranquillity are lovely mind states, and, indeed, they share the quality of evenness, smoothness. This element of serenity is an important factor in the mind, balancing vigor, interest, and rapture so that clear seeing and understanding can emerge. But calmness and tranquillity aren't the goal of practice, at least not for me. I want to be able to get excited. The more I realize that everything is empty and meaningless unless we imbue it with significance, the more I want to be able to imbue. Here I am in a life. I want to *remember* that it's only a movie, and I want to *live* it as if it's real.

Eight years ago, on the afternoon of the day on which I was scheduled to begin teaching our longest retreat of the year in California, my daughter Emily unexpectedly dropped by to visit.

"Would you and Dad like to take Johan and me out to dinner tonight?" she asked.

"We would, but I can't because the retreat begins tonight, and I need to teach," I explained.

"Are you *sure* you don't want to go to dinner?"

"No, I *do* want to go to dinner, but I can't because I am teaching."

"You can't even go out to celebrate that you're going to be a grandmother for the first time?"

I shrieked with joy. I was beside myself. I jumped up and down. In the middle of this the phone rang, and I picked it up. It was my friend Alta. "I can't talk," I said, "I'm hysterical!"

Afterward, Emily laughed and said, "I'm so sorry I didn't bring a video camera." All four of us went to dinner. Then I went to the retreat and taught the first class.

I have become more passionate, not less. When I am delighted, which is often, I am ecstatic. When I am sad, I cry easily. Nothing is a big deal. It's whatever it is, and then it's something else.

Done Is Done

•

One of my first Buddhist teachers used a three-word phrase when he wanted me to pay attention to the present moment. "Done is done," he would say. Coming into the final stages of writing this book, I wondered how I'd know when I was done. I love telling stories, and every day is a new story.

I recalled a conversation I once had with Jack, another trusted teacher and my good friend.

"I'm worried that I've lost my spiritual zeal," I said to him. "I think I understand the formula for happiness. I'm positive I'll have to practice it the whole rest of my life, but I don't feel I need to ask more questions."

"Sounds right to me," he replied. "When you've gotten the message, you hang up the phone."

I had two messages to deliver in this book. The first is about spiritual living. I think it's plain. Ordinary people do it, and they don't even know they are doing it. In the middle of plain lives, with regular joys and griefs, they live with grace and kindness and are happy.

The second message is about wisdom teachers. They are all over the place. I noticed as this book evolved that many of my teachers were people in airplanes. I briefly considered some esoteric symbolic significance like, "airplanes move you to new places" or "airplanes rise up high," but I knew that was extra mind-embroidery. I have many airplane teachers because I'm in airplanes a lot. *Everybody* is a teacher. "Pay attention to everyone *always*," I think, "because everyone is something of a Buddha."

The reverse of Jack's advice is also true. "When you've given the message, you hang up the phone." I think I've done it.

ALTA'S MARINATED MUSHROOMS

Whisk together:

> 2/3 cup olive oil
> 1/3 cup seasoned rice vinegar
> 2 teaspoons soy sauce
> 1/2 teaspoon Mongolian Fire Oil (or 1/4 teaspoon cayenne)
> 1 tablespoon chopped fresh parsley

Parboil 1 to 1-1/2 pounds of mushrooms. Pour marinade over them while they are still hot. Marinate for at least one hour, spooning marinade over them occasionally.

Optional variation: Purple onions, sliced thin, may be included and may be added with the marinade. One red pepper, chopped, is another good addition.

The mushrooms should be served within four hours.

For more information about Insight Meditation, contact:

Spirit Rock Meditation Center
5000 Sir Francis Drake Blvd.
Box 909C
Woodacre, CA 94973
(415) 488-0164

Insight Meditation Society
1230 Pleasant Street
Barre, MA 01005
(508) 355-4378

Tapes and books are available through:

Dharma Seed Tape Library
PO Box 66
Wendell Depot, MA 01380
(800) 969-7333